D1516522

"*God's Plan for You: Life, Love, M* ... most welcome book. In language ... people, the author gently leads his readers into a healthy understanding of human sexuality. Pope John Paul II's *Theology of the Body* is made not only accessible, but inviting for young people. The author's use of Scripture helps the reader connect theology and revelation. His ample use of anecdotes and examples anchors the truths of faith in life. A great book. A most useful tool."

— Most Rev. Arthur J. Serratelli
Bishop of Paterson, New Jersey
Chairman of the Committee on Doctrine
U.S. Catholic Bishops

"I really enjoyed reading *God's Plan for You*. In it, David takes the beautiful teachings of our Church and the words of Pope John Paul the Great and puts them in terms that all can understand. This book beautifully weaves together God's great design for life, love, marriage, and sex. I appreciated the fact that David always refers back to Scripture and the *Catechism of the Catholic Church* as the basis for each of his points. Young people today are struggling to hear and really live the truth. This book boldly and yet lovingly lays out God's truth. I thank David for giving me a great resource which I can use with the campus ministry program that my wife and I lead in our home town."

— Tony Melendez
Composer and musician

"In a world that bombards all of us, and particularly young people, with deceptive and confusing messages about the gift of our sexuality, David has put together an indispensable resource. His humor and personality shine through even as he deals with difficult topics, and the message is *right on the money*. He has brought both *The Theology of the Body* and Church teaching in the *Catechism* into clear focus and everyday language. I am inspired by this book, knowing the power that it has to change lives."

— Steve Angrisano
Youth minister, singer, and songwriter

God's
plan
for you

Life, Love, Marriage & Sex

By David Hajduk

Illustrated by Norman Dapito

Foreword by Mary Beth Bonacci

Pauline
BOOKS & MEDIA
Boston

Nihil Obstat: Reverend Christopher J. Kirwan, Jr., D.T.M.
Imprimatur: ✠ Archbishop Seán O'Malley, OFM Cap.
Archbishop of Boston
January 10, 2006

Library of Congress Cataloging-in-Publication Data

Hajduk, David (David Charles)
  God's plan for you : life, love, marriage, and sex / David Hajduk.
    p. cm.
  Includes bibliographical references.
  ISBN 0-8198-4517-5 (pbk.)
  1. Marriage—Religious aspects—Catholic Church. 2. Sex—Religious aspects—
Catholic Church. 3. Catholic Church—Doctrines. 4. Teenagers—Sexual behav-
ior. 5. Teenagers—Conduct of life. 6. Teenagers—Religious life. I. Title.
  BX2250.H26 2006
  248.8'3—dc22

                          2005019276

Scripture texts in this work, unless otherwise noted, are from the Catholic Edition of the *Revised Standard Version of the Bible*, copyright 1965, 1966 by the Division of Christian Education of the National Council of the Churches of Christ in the United States of America. Used by permission. All rights reserved.

All Papal quotations used with the permission of the Libreria Editrice Vaticana, 00120, Città del Vaticano.

Excerpts from the English translation of the *Catechism of the Catholic Church* for use in the United States of America, copyright © 1994, United States Catholic Conference, Inc. — Libreria Editrice Vaticana. Used with permission.

The BURGER KING® trademark is used with permission from Burger King Brands, Inc.

Cover design by Rosana Usselmann

Cover photo by photospin, © 2006, www.photospin.com

Artwork by Norman Dapito, copyright © 2006, Daughters of St. Paul

"P" and PAULINE are registered trademarks of the Daughters of St. Paul.

Copyright © 2006, David Charles Hajduk

Published by Pauline Books & Media, 50 Saint Paul's Avenue, Boston, MA 02130-3491. www.pauline.org.

Printed in U.S.A.

Pauline Books & Media is the publishing house of the Daughters of St. Paul, an international congregation of women religious serving the Church with the com-munications media.

3 4 5 6 7 8 9   13 12 11 10 09

For my father, the "man behind the man,"
who by his words and example
has taught me what it means
to love as God loves.

Contents

Acknowledgments

I would like to thank the following people and groups of people, who are all truly collaborators in the work you hold in your hands:

Jesus Christ, for my life and all that's in it, and for being a patient and loving Savior as I myself came to learn, at times "kicking and screaming," the truths that I have presented in this book.

Pope John Paul II, who in such a real and powerful way was the Vicar of Christ for me, and taught me more about life, love, marriage, and sex than anyone else on earth.

Shannon, my wife and true companion, for all that we have built and continue to build by God's grace, for our common life and mission, for being my "helper" and loving me so freely, totally, faithfully, and fruitfully each and every day, for being such a devoted "mother and teacher" to our children, and for being the best proofreader and reviewer that any author has ever known.

My children: Miranda, Daniel, Emily, Jamie, John Paul, and Benjamin, who continued to show encouragement and excitement about this project, even though it meant days when Daddy may have seemed to spend more time with the computer than with them. I definitely owe you guys a few hours coloring, drawing, making crafts, playing games, and reading *The Lord of the Rings!*

My parents, for providing for my needs, for always believing that I could accomplish great things if I worked hard, and for being unwavering in their thinking that I'm the best thing since sliced bread.

My friends, who believed in me and who, if they ever got tired of discussing the book, never once let on.

The monks of St. Mary's Abbey-Delbarton School, for assigning me the Family Life class to teach, for providing me with the opportunity to further my studies, and for the many and varied ways in which they have embodied Benedictine hospitality for my family.

All the professors and administrators at Immaculate Conception Seminary, South Orange, New Jersey—especially Rev. Anthony Ziccardi, S.T.L., Rev. Joseph Chapel, S.T.D., Rev. Anthony Figueiredo, S.T.D., Deacon Bill Toth, Ph.D., and Ms. Dianne Traflet, S.T.D.—who, in addition to their knowledge, have imparted their friendship to me.

Marie Ryan, the Director of Family Life for the Diocese of Paterson, New Jersey, for her personal support and encouragement, and for enthusiastically promoting my work while always remaining sensitive to my vocation as a husband and father.

The religious educators and youth ministers who reviewed my initial manuscript, believed in the value of the project, and offered their professional advice: Catzel Bumpus, Courtney Fleming, Joel Peters, Michael St. Pierre, and Allan Wright.

All the young people I have had the pleasure to teach or minister to over the years, who, whether they knew it or not, were actually teaching and ministering to me; and for those specific young people who took such great interest in this project, looked over the different chapters, and honestly shared their opinion about what worked and what didn't.

Norm Dapito, for his incredible artistic talents and for the many in-depth conversations we have had about *Star Wars*...among other things.

Mary Beth Bonacci, for taking time out of her busy schedule to write the foreword.

Pauline Books & Media and their associates—especially Sr. Donna, Sr. Marianne Lorraine, and Mr. Steven Colella—for believing in this project, for their expert advice, and for sharing a passion and vision for reaching young people with the life-giving message of God's original plan for life, love, marriage, and sex!

Foreword

Pope John Paul II changed my life.

When I first heard of his Theology of the Body, I was a senior in college and a "nice Catholic girl." By that, I mean that I went to Mass on Sunday and tried to avoid committing the really big sins. I followed the rules because I knew they were the rules. I have to admit, I wasn't entirely sure *why* they were the rules, or why I was supposed to follow them. I knew I wasn't supposed to steal or kill, because that hurt people. And I abstained from sexual activity because I didn't want to get pregnant and didn't want to make God mad.

Compelling, but not particularly positive reasons.

All of that changed when a series of four speakers came in to talk to us about John Paul II and the Theology of the Body. I was completely blown away. I saw "the rules" in a whole new light. God's laws—his morality—are about *love!* He has a plan for our lives and for our bodies. When he says "Thou shalt not..." it's because if we "shalt," we'll end up hurting ourselves and hurting our ability to love.

I saw in particular how the Catholic Church's teaching on human sexuality was based in love. We're created for love. We hunger for love. And we think somehow that "making love" will help us to live love.

It doesn't work that way. Living God's plan—chastity—helps us find and live love.

I thought this news was so exciting, I decided I wanted to share it with teenagers. I've been doing that full time ever since.

John Paul II had an amazing gift for conveying the truths of our faith in a beautiful, positive way. He made Christ's love so real and so immediate that rules didn't seem like rules anymore. They were simply a natural response to God's overwhelming love for us.

From the very beginning of my work with teens and chastity, everything I've said or written has been based in the Theology of the Body. I didn't go out of my way to advertise that fact in the early years of my ministry, because the word "theology" freaked people out. But JPII changed even that. Now the Theology of the Body is actually "cool." People are excited about it; they want to learn about it.

Fortunately, you have an excellent opportunity to do just that. David Hajduk shares my enthusiasm for the work of John Paul II, and he has captured the Holy Father's message in the book you hold in your hands. Take full advantage of this opportunity. Read it. Re-read it. Think about it. Pray to understand it on a deeper and deeper level.

John Paul II's signature phrase was "Be not afraid." I want you to remember that as you read this book. God is madly in love with you. He wants what is best for you. Most of all, God wants to have a relationship with you. He wants you to share eternal happiness with him in heaven.

God is on your side. And that, my friends, is very, very good news.

Read on....

MARY BETH BONACCI

CHAPTER 1

The Cosmic Prequel

> Some Pharisees approached him, and tested him, saying, "Is it lawful for a man to divorce his wife for any cause whatever?" He said in reply, "Have you not read that from the beginning the Creator 'made them male and female' and said, 'For this reason a man shall leave his father and mother and be joined to his wife, and the two shall become one flesh'? So they are no longer two, but one flesh. Therefore, what God has joined together, no human being must separate."
>
> — Matthew 19:3–6 NAB

God's Plan for You from "the Beginning"

The first *Star Wars* movie (which was really the fourth) came out when I was in the first grade, and I eagerly awaited each subsequent episode. My father and I would stand in lines that wrapped around the movie theater and continued for blocks. I had every action figure, as well as the Darth Vader carrying case. I had all the spaceships. I traded *Star Wars* cards. You get the picture.

So in 1999, when George Lucas began coming out with the prequels, "the story behind the story," I was pumped up beyond your wildest imagination. I immediately changed from a thirty-year-old man back into a seven-year-old boy, and all was right with the world. My kids instantly morphed into *Star Wars* junkies. The hours spent jumping around the living room recreating the light saber "dual of the fates" between Darth Maul, Qui-Gon Jinn, and Obi-wan Kenobi will be forever etched in our memories.

Whatever you may think of the *Star Wars* movies, one thing is fair to say: the movies that I saw growing up—the saga of Darth Vader, Luke Skywalker, and Princess Leia—are just plain easier to understand because the prequels have now been made. Let's just say that watching them I have experienced my share of "a-ha" moments: moments when a lightbulb went on in my head and I suddenly realized something I hadn't before. Well, when Jesus refers the Pharisees back to "the beginning," to the time when God created human beings and the first human couple, you might say he is reminding them about their "prequel," about the story behind their story. And since their prequel is everybody's prequel—including yours and mine—you could call it *The Cosmic Prequel.*

Why would Jesus want to take the Pharisees and us back to the beginning and remind us about the story behind our story? Because Jesus wants us to understand what our lives are really all about. He wants us to know God's plan for us, and he wants us to see how the amazing gifts of love, marriage, and sex are all part of that plan! I really do believe that Jesus hoped (and still hopes) that doing so would create for us some serious "a-ha" moments.

Pope John Paul II hoped so too! That's why, at the beginning of his pontificate, he devoted over five years' worth of general audience teachings to *The Cosmic Prequel* and how it sheds light on love, marriage, and sex. This teaching eventually became known as the *Theology of the Body*. In it he stresses the goodness of the body and how a proper understanding of the body enables us to know what it means to be human and what human sexuality is all about. This brings me to the book you have in your hands.

> **WORD to the WISE**
>
> **Pontificate** is a fancy word meaning the Holy Father's time as **pope.**

> **Did U Know**
>
> The custom of a **general audience** (abbreviated as GA in this book), a weekly teaching given by the Holy Father, was started by Pope Pius IX in the 1870s.

The Meaning of Life, Love, Marriage, and Sex, and the Pope from Poland

Have you ever wondered what life is all about? Have you ever struggled with finding your place in this world? Have you ever looked in a mirror and been unsure if you like what you see, or even *know* what you see? Have you ever been confused about relationships, sex, or members of the opposite sex? Have you become disillusioned about marriage and family life? Well, you're not alone. When I was a teen, I did my share of questioning, and in my years working with teens I have never met one who hasn't wrestled with these issues on some level.

The teenage years can be difficult, and even more so today. Enormous pressure, great expectations, and an uncertain future cause great stress. Scholar, athlete, artist, or none of the above—practically no one can escape the "college crunch." We supposedly live in the Information Age, but we're fed so much contradictory information that it's hard to know what to believe about anything.

Then there are those guy-girl relationships. As far as sex goes, who knows what to think anymore? Parents and Church say, "Just say no," and MTV and VH1 say, "Just do it" ("Just wear a condom"). Eating disorders, drinking binges, pot smoking, rave parties, date rapes, sexually transmitted diseases, abortions, and the like spread more and more, yet society seems to be able to offer little in terms of concrete answers to such problems. As divorces increase, many teens look at their own broken families and ask, "Is this the best I can hope for?"

How could an old Polish man who lived in the Vatican for over twenty-six years possibly have known anything about your life, your struggles, your hopes, dreams, or fears? Yet he did. It may

surprise you to learn that as a young man he dreamed of becoming a famous actor in the theater. As a young priest, he worked with youth and spent lots of time with them, taking them on canoeing, hiking, and skiing trips (John Paul used to be quite an avid skier). As pope, he loved to meet with young people from all over the globe at the World Youth Day celebrations every two years. He really did love young people and cared very deeply for them. He really did understand. And from heaven he really wants *you* to live life to the full and not to fear the future.

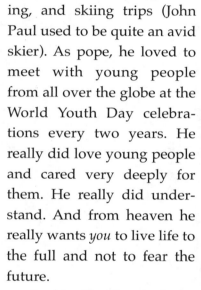

Notable Quotable

"You are young, and the Pope is old; 82 or 83 years of life is not the same as 22 or 23. But the Pope still fully identifies with your hopes and aspirations. Although I have lived through much darkness, under harsh totalitarian regimes, I have seen enough evidence to be unshakably convinced that no difficulty, no fear is so great that it can completely suffocate the hope that springs eternal in the hearts of the young. You, the young, are our hope. Do not let that hope die! Stake your lives on it!"
—Pope John Paul II

In his Theology of the Body, John Paul II has provided us with the secret to a full life and a reason to hope for the future. In it we find the purpose of our existence, and the answers to our most deeply held questions about life, relationships, and sexuality. And it really is some of the most powerful, uplifting, and downright mind-blowing stuff on earth! It makes what a consumerist or purely secular society offers seem like nothing but the utter fake that it is.

I only wish that I had learned about it before my mid-twenties. It would have spared me a lot of confusion, pain, and bad choices. That's why I want to introduce it to you. That's precisely why I wrote this book.

How to Get the Most from This Book

In the following pages, I have broken the Theology of the Body down into bite-size portions. Each chapter begins with an important insight from God's Word as the "springboard" for that chapter's theme. Please read it slowly and prayerfully. Then, I offer an introductory example or analogy, and present one piece of *The Cosmic Prequel* and what it teaches us about the meaning of life, love, marriage, and sex. Each chapter ends with an "In His Own Words" section containing a quote from Pope John Paul II on that chapter's topic; a "Things to Ponder and Share" section with questions that will help you relate the themes discussed in the chapter to your everyday life; and some suggested reading from the *Catechism of the Catholic Church (CCC)* to help you to "go deeper" if you so choose. All in all, I have written the book like I speak, in the hopes that it will read less like a textbook and more like a conversation with a friend.

So, let's take a look at *The Cosmic Prequel*—the story behind our story. Those "a-ha" moments are waiting for us.

JOHN PAUL II
In His Own Words

Those who seek the accomplishment of their own human and Christian vocation in marriage are called, first of all, to make the theology of the body...the content of their life and behavior.

(*GA*, 4/2/80)

Things to Ponder and Share

1. Understanding "the story behind our story" helps us to understand and appreciate our story. Have you ever wondered about your family history: where your relatives came from and when, what perhaps earlier generations did when they got to this country, etc.? Ask your parents or grandparents about it the next time you get a chance. You'll be fascinated by the stories!

2. What are the reasons Jesus takes the Pharisees (and us) back to "the beginning"?

3. What pressures face teens today? How do you cope with them?

4. What is the world's attitude toward relationships, sex, and marriage? What are some

subtle and not so subtle examples that
demonstrate it?

5. Who is the pope in your own words? Have you
ever thought about him caring for you personally? Why or why not?

6. What are some of the questions you or other
young people today might have about love,
marriage, and sex? Do you think Pope John
Paul II might have some answers to those
questions in his Theology of the Body?
Why?

Read the
Catechism of the Catholic Church

nos. 1701, 1602–1603

CHAPTER 2

The Key to a Rich Life

"Do not lay up for yourselves treasures on earth, where moth and rust consume and where thieves break in and steal, but lay up for yourselves treasures in heaven, where neither moth nor rust consumes and where thieves do not break in and steal. For where your treasure is, there will your heart be also."

— Matthew 6:19–21

Life's Most Important Questions

The movie *It's a Wonderful Life* starring Jimmy Stewart brings a tear to my eye every time I watch it. If you have never seen it, don't worry—it's on TV at least a hundred times from Thanksgiving to Christmas. It tells the story of George Bailey, a man of duty and charity who meets hard times. He stands to lose his reputation, family welfare, and business because his archrival, a heartless and crooked old miser named Mr. Potter, wants to ruin him. Unlike George, Mr. Potter has no concern for the hardworking men and women in town and views them solely as a means of profit. Desperate,

George begins to think that he is worth more dead than alive and that everyone would be better off if he had never been born. Well, through the intervention of a second-class angel trying to earn his wings, George gets the chance to see what life would have been like had he never existed, and he realizes all the wonderful things he has done with his life. The movie ends at George's house, as all the people that George had helped rally together to help him in his time of need. George's brother, Harry, shows up and proposes a toast: "To my brother, George Bailey— the richest man in town!"

Everyone wants to have a rich life. Everyone wants to "store up treasure for themselves." However, the real question is: What makes a person rich? At some point in life, everyone will have to answer this question for him or herself—and the answer will ultimately determine how full his or her life will be.

At its core, the question "What makes a person rich?" inquires into the meaning of life and the purpose of human existence. In a sense, it asks two separate yet related questions: "Who am I?" and "What's life all about?" Our life hinges on these two questions—the most important questions that any human being can ask. Somehow we know that our personal happiness depends on finding the answers; that if we only knew what life was really about, then we would have the roadmap to fulfillment in our lives. That's why we have a natural inclination to search. However, we often search in all the wrong places. We can go the way of Mr. Potter or the way of George Bailey.

People have been asking "Who am I?" and "What's life all about?" ever since Adam and Eve. Because so many people before you have wrestled with these questions, you can benefit from their hard work. Of all the great thinkers, however, the famous Greek philosopher Aristotle said it best.

The Way to True Happiness

Thousands of years ago, in his work *Nicomachean Ethics*, Aristotle said that the meaning of life is to be happy, and that ultimately happiness is the thing that everybody is searching for. However, Aristotle meant something very specific by happiness. For Aristotle, "happiness" means "fulfillment." Understood this way, happiness refers to an internal condition whose opposite is *emptiness*—not sadness, suffering, or pain as many might think. Happiness is a deep sense of peace and contentment in one's soul. This means it can actually *co-exist* with sadness, suffering, and pain. Your world could be falling apart and you could be enduring great trials, yet you can still feel content and peaceful in your heart because you are *fulfilled*. True happiness, therefore, doesn't come and go; it is enduring. And this is precisely the happiness that everybody longs for. Those who say

> **WORD to the WISE**
>
> The word Aristotle used for happiness, *eudemonia*, translates more literally as "fulfillment."

things like, "I'll only be happy if I get that car, go to that college, or get that girlfriend or boyfriend," or "I'll only be happy if my lousy circumstances change," sadly don't understand what true happiness is and are only setting themselves up to be disappointed. True happiness happens from the inside out, not the outside in. This is why Aristotle said that there are three main ways in which people tend to seek happiness. Mr. Potter exemplifies the first two, and George Bailey the third.

The first is the way of pleasure. This way promises fulfillment by pleasing the senses and avoiding pain at all costs. It involves lots of eating, drinking, and sex; always looking toward the new and improved "high." It looks no farther than the next party. Aristotle called those who seek fulfillment in this way "vulgar" and "animalistic." He wasn't trying to be mean—he was simply stating that those who live this life lower themselves to the level of animals. Aristotle concluded that such people will never find the fulfillment they seek. If you look at people who seem to have all the pleasure they want, yet still seem unhappy and empty inside, you'll see that Aristotle was right.

The second is the way of power. This way promises fulfillment from being popular and having many possessions. It's all about stardom and stuff. In the eyes of the world, these things make a person powerful. They unlock the door to all the fine food, strong drink, hard drugs, sex, and material possessions that one could possibly imagine. In this sense, the life of power merely provides the means to the life of pleasure. Like those who seek the life of pleasure, those who seek the life of power don't find the fulfillment they seek either. Popularity evaporates, here one minute and gone the next. It depends on others' opinions of you, after all, and you cannot control that. Money can run out; the stock market can crash; thieves can "break in and steal." What then?

The third is the way of virtue. This way promises fulfillment from living a morally good life. The word *virtue* comes from the Latin word *vir,* meaning "man." So, virtue literally means "manliness" or "humanliness." Virtue is human perfection. *Being virtuous means being human.* Think about those we honor in history as great people, as opposed to those we revile as scoundrels. Isn't virtue the criterion? We call them great people because they represent the best that humans have to offer, because they exemplify everything we aspire to be.

Notable Quotable

"...Virtuous activities and their opposites are what constitute happiness or the reverse."
— Aristotle

So, what was Aristotle's conclusion? *Human fulfillment results from being fully human.* If you want to be happy, then you've got to be human. Only then will you be truly rich.

Now, you may ask, "What does it really mean to be human?" *The first lesson that Jesus teaches us from*

The Cosmic Prequel answers this great question. Jesus knows that we can't even begin to understand what human love, human sexuality, marriage, and family life are all about—let alone find fulfillment in them—until we first understand what being human is all about.

Let's go back to the beginning with Jesus and discover what God had in mind when he created us. The key to a rich life is just around the corner!

JOHN PAUL II
In His Own Words

Happiness is being rooted in love.

(*GA*, 1/30/80)

Things to Ponder and Share

1. Look at your life and the world around you. Do you know someone like George Bailey?

2. If you were asked to give your "Life Motto" —a phrase that sums up who you are and what your life is about—what would it be and why?

3. How did Aristotle understand happiness?
   How do many people today understand it?
   What's the difference?

4. According to Aristotle, what are the three
   different types of lives that humans can lead
   to try to find fulfillment? What was his conclusion? Do you agree? Why or why not?

5. When have you pursued happiness in pleasure,
   popularity, or possessions? How did it turn
   out in the short term? In the long term?

6. Who do you think are the great human beings
   in our world's history? What made them great?

Read the ─────────────────────────

Catechism of the Catholic Church

nos. 27, 1718, 1723, 1803   ◄─────────────

CHAPTER 3

A **Striking**
Similarity

Then God said, "Let us make man in our image, after our likeness; and let them have dominion over the fish of the sea, and over the birds of the air, and over the cattle, and over all the earth, and over every creeping thing that creeps upon the earth." So God created man in his own image, in the image of God he created him; male and female he created them. And God blessed them, and God said to them, "Be fruitful and multiply, and fill the earth and subdue it; and have dominion over the fish of the sea and over the birds of the air and over every living thing that moves upon the earth."

> **Did U Know**
> The word "man" can refer to a male human being or to humanity as a whole—both men and women. The latter is how it is intended here. This is important to keep in mind as you read quotes from Scripture or from Pope John Paul II.

— Genesis 1:26–28

Created in the Image and Likeness of God

One of my favorite books when I was a small boy was *Are You My Mother?* by P. D. Eastman. Maybe you've read it. It's a story about a little bird that

19

hatches while his mother is away from the nest gathering food. When he breaks out of his egg, his first instinct is to identify his mother. Realizing that she is not there, he decides to go looking for her. But since he doesn't know what his mother looks like, he travels from creature to creature and thing to thing asking the question: "Are you my mother?" The book then recounts the perilous adventures of this poor little bird as he searches for his mommy.

For whatever reason, this book reached into my heart when I was a little boy. Maybe I felt as though I could identify with this little bird, since I had gotten lost my share of times in the local department store and had felt that hole in the pit of my stomach as I frantically looked for my parents up and down every aisle. Or maybe it was simply because I had a deep sense of compassion for him. After all, he was all alone, separated from his mother, and since he didn't know where he came from, he had no idea what he was. Talk about an identity crisis.

The climactic event of the story comes when the little guy meets the "Snort," which is really a huge construction crane, and it unexpectedly places him back into his nest. At that very moment, the mother bird returns. She asks her little one, "Do you know who I am?" The birdie replies, "You are not a kitten. You are not a hen. You are not a dog. You are not a cow. You are not a boat, or a plane, or a Snort! You are a bird, and you are my mother." And the two presumably live happily ever after.

Well, believe it or not, we have a lot in common with that little bird. The truth is that if we are going to know who we are as human beings, we are first going to have to know where we come from. And that's exactly why the first passage that Jesus refers to in his response to the Pharisees' question about divorce is the creation story of Genesis 1.

This passage makes it resoundingly clear that we come from God and that we are created in *his image and likeness*. Now, of course, to be made in God's image and likeness doesn't mean to be God himself. As creatures, we are much more *unlike* than like God. Yet, the revelation that we are made in the image of God gives us the key to unlocking the meaning and purpose of our existence. If we could know *who God is*, then we could discover *who we are*. Theodicy (the study of what it means to be God) precedes anthropology (the study of what it means to be human). So, based on what the Scriptures tell us about who God is, what do we learn about who we are as creatures made in God's image and likeness?

Persons Who Can Think and Choose

First, we can see that God is a thinking-choosing sort of being. Notice in the passage how deliberately he chooses to create the world, especially human beings: "Let us make man in our image, after our likeness; and let them have dominion over the fish of the sea, and over the birds of the air, and over the cattle, and over all the earth, and over every creeping thing that creeps upon the earth" (Gen 1:26). What is also striking is that God is clearly a rational being. He has thought through exactly what he is going to do, and then he does it.

Thus, the first thing it means to be made in the image of God is that, like God, *we are a thinking-choosing sort of being*. And we have a name we give to thinking-choosing beings: we call them *persons*. Persons can think and choose, precisely because they have the "powers" to do so; that is, they have *intellects* and they have *wills*. These powers give them some unique capacities. For one, they are the only beings that are *free* or "in charge" of themselves. That means that persons alone are capable of determining who they are and who they will become by their own free choices. In addition, since persons are *free* or "in charge" of themselves, they are the only beings that can truly *give* themselves to another person or persons. This is because gifts, by their very nature, must always be free.

It should be mentioned here that it's not that someone actually has use of all these powers and capacities that makes him or her a person. It is that someone is *the sort of being* that has these powers and capacities that makes him or her a person. This is a crucial distinction. Otherwise, we would have to say that infants and those with certain disabilities aren't persons at all, which of course is absurd.

Because persons have intellects and wills, are free and "in charge" of themselves, and can give themselves to another person or persons, they are also capable of love. In fact, the very reason persons have these powers and capacities is *so* they can love. And this leads to the second thing it means to be made in the image of God: *we were made to love as God loves.*

Made for True Love

In the Scriptures, whenever we find the word "love" referring to God, it's always a certain kind of love; a love traditionally called *charity.* You could say that charity is "God's brand" of love. This means that charity is the "true love" we were made for! It is defined as *freely giving oneself for the good of another,* that is, for another's *own sake.* Now, let's break down the definition piece by piece.

"Freely"—This means that love is something *chosen* or *willed.* Love is primarily a decision we make, not a feeling or an emotion. Our feelings and emotions may "move" us to want to choose the good of another or may even accompany such a choice. However, experience shows that this isn't always the case. That's why real love is in the choosing, not in the feeling. This is not to say that love is emotion*less* or that there is no such thing as a feeling of love. Such emotions and feelings are very real and rooted in human nature. However, they are only good if they motivate us to choose what is good—which is what they should do. That's why it's the job of our intellects to determine

if our emotions and feelings are compatible with what is truly good (see *Catechism of the Catholic Church*, nos. 1766–1770).

"Giving oneself"—This means that love is not merely the gift of a person's care and concern; it is the gift of the very person. Love doesn't so much give some*thing* as it gives some*one!* You may not think that you are giving yourself to your parents when you're washing the dishes or taking out the garbage, but, assuming that you are doing it willfully, that is exactly what you are doing. And since love means *giving* oneself, *it always involves sacrifice.* The greatness of the love is determined by the willingness to sacrifice, which is nothing other than the amount one is willing to give of him- or herself. That's what makes Jesus' love so huge (see Jn 15:13 and Rom 5:8).

"For the good of another"—Notice the definite article: *the* good. This indicates that *what is good* is not a matter of opinion or personal feelings, but is rather something *objectively true* that is *known* by the *intellect.* You can't have "true love" without "the truth." It also indicates that love is *choosing what is good,* in particular what is good for another person. And this sometimes doesn't feel particularly good at all. In fact, it can entail great suffering—like enduring the ridicule of your peers because you stand up for the kid who is being picked on. However, accepting personal suffering for doing what is good is the very "stuff" of love.

The Qualities of God's Brand of Love

Now, God's brand of love (or charity) also has certain distinguishing qualities. It is *free, total, faithful,* and *fruitful*.[1]

First, God's love is *free*. This means that God *chooses* to love—it is not something that is somehow out of his control. I have often heard people say, "You can't help whom you love," but that's really not the case. You may not be able to choose how you feel about someone, but you can certainly choose whether or not to give yourself for that person's good.

> **Did U Know**
> These four characteristics of God's love—that it is free, total, faithful, and fruitful—are found in Pope Paul VI's landmark encyclical *Of Human Life*, in which he describes marital love as a reflection of God's love.

Being free, God's love, however, could also mean that it doesn't cost anything. God gives it freely, whether or not the one loved receives it, returns it, or even deserves it. Why, you ask? Because God wills what is good for every person, all the time, no matter what. This is what is meant by the popular phrase "God's love is unconditional"— there's nothing you can do to make him stop willing what is good for you!

Second, God's love is *total*. This means that God gives himself completely for the good and enrichment of another, without reservation or selfish ulterior motives. That's why God's love is sometimes called a "disinterested" love. It's not that he's not interested in you; it's that he is *so interested* in you and your good that his "own interests" don't really factor in.

Third, God's love is *faithful*. This means that God's love endures forever, even in spite of the unfaithfulness of the one loved. Do you know how when someone wants to prove that what he or she is saying is true, that person may swear an oath to God? A good example is a witness in a court of law. The reason he or she swears to tell the truth "so help me God" is that there's no authority higher than God. Well, in speaking to Abraham, God actually swears an oath to himself! He says to Abraham, "By myself I have sworn" (see Gen 22:16). That was God's way of saying "You can trust me to keep my promises." He is truth itself, after all.

Finally, God's love is *fruitful*. This means that God's love always seeks to give life and include others in it. God never intentionally sterilizes his love. God's love is a *generous love*. It not only gives physical life and spiritual life, it fosters, sustains, and encourages the *fullness of life*. God creating the world and caring for his creation—especially human beings—should be proof of that! Jesus himself said, "I came that they may have life, and have it *abundantly*" (Jn 10:10, my italics). And God's love is *radically inclusive*. The more people there are to share in his love, the "merrier," so to speak. With God, there's always enough love to go around!

Now, you may be thinking to yourself: "Hey, this sounds a lot like the qualities of married love."

And you'd be right. Married love is one of the greatest earthly examples of God's love precisely because it shares these qualities so fully. Yet, if all human beings are made to love as God loves, then *all human love*—whether it's the love shown to a spouse, a parent, a child, a friend, or even a stranger—must embody these qualities in some fashion.

Getting Connected: Made for Communion

When persons give themselves freely, totally, faithfully, and fruitfully for each other's good, they become *spiritually united* or "connected" with one another. That is, they form what is called a *communion of persons*. And this leads to the third thing it means to be made in the image of God: *we were made for a communion of persons*. You could say that to be human means to "get connected."

It is the Christian belief that God himself is a communion of persons! This is what the doctrine of the Holy Trinity is all about. God is *three Persons*— the Father, the Son, and the Holy Spirit—*in one God*. God is three distinct persons who share a common nature, and are completely one with each other because of their mutual love. The Father loves the Son from all eternity. He gives himself freely, totally, faithfully, and fruitfully to the Son for his Son's own sake. The Son receives and accepts the gift of the Father. He then returns the Father's total self-giving with his own and gives himself freely, totally, faith-

fully, and fruitfully to the Father for his Father's own sake. Since the gift that is given from the Father to the Son and from the Son to the Father *is God* (the total self-gift of God would necessarily be God), then the Gift itself, the Love between the Father and the Son, is another Divine Person. We call that Person the Holy Spirit.

It is easy to see, therefore, what St. John meant when he wrote those famous words, "God is love" (1 Jn 4:8). You could really say that God is one big love-fest. But you could also say that God is one big *life*-fest. The Father's love gives birth to the Son; from the love of the Father and the Son the Spirit is conceived; and by the free choice of the life-giving communion of persons we call the Trinity, the universe is created.

Coming Attractions

As we will see later on, the most fundamental example of a life-giving communion of persons is marriage and the family.

So, being made in the image of the Trinity means that we are made for a life-giving communion of persons too! In fact, this is the ultimate way in which we image God, because it is the whole point of being persons who can "freely give themselves for the good of one another."

With all this said, here is a good definition of human beings:

> *Human beings,*
> *as persons created in the image of God,*
> *are endowed with intellects and wills,*
> *so they can make the free, total, faithful,*
> *and fruitful gift of themselves for each other's good*
> *and thus form a communion of persons.*

You could say that we bear a striking similarity to God. Yet, although God and we are similar in that we are persons who are oriented toward love and communion, God is pure spirit (as are the angels) and we aren't. We have bodies. God made us "body-persons," who are both matter and spirit. And this is what makes us one of a kind in all of creation. We are "the best of both worlds."

JOHN PAUL II
In His Own Words

Right "from the beginning" he [man] is... essentially an image of an [unfathomable] divine communion of persons. This same man, willed by the Creator in this way right from "the beginning," can find himself only in the disinterested giving of himself.

For Your Consideration

Brackets in a quote mean that the words are mine and are used to clarify a speaker's identity or to make a word or phrase more understandable.

(*GA*, 11/14/79 and 1/16/80)

Things to Ponder and Share

1. Think of a time in your life when you faced an "identity crisis"—when you seriously questioned who you were or who you were becoming. How did you resolve it?

2. What are the three ways we bear a striking similarity to God? Briefly explain each.

3. What is a simple definition of love? Define the three pieces of this simple definition. How is it different from the ways love is commonly understood?

4. What are some concrete ways you can freely give yourself for the good of your parents? Your grandparents? Your brothers and sisters? Your friends? Your church? Your town? The poor, lonely, or those treated unfairly?

5. Think about a time in your life when you loved or failed to love unconditionally, disinterestedly, faithfully, or inclusively.

6. What does the phrase "communion of persons" mean? What are some examples of such "communions"?

Read the
Catechism of the Catholic Church

nos. 356–358, 1702–1705, 1766, 2331

CHAPTER 4

The Best of Both Worlds

...[T]hen the LORD God formed man of dust from the ground, and breathed into his nostrils the breath of life; and man became a living being. And the LORD God planted a garden in Eden, in the east; and there he put the man whom he had formed.

— Genesis 2:7–8

Body and Soul

If you have ever watched those television shows on classic TV commercials, then you have probably seen the ones from the '70s for Reese's peanut butter cups. They always showed the fateful meeting of two unsuspecting people, one with a chocolate bar and one with a tub of peanut butter. As they minded their own business, suddenly, through some accident, apparent tragedy would strike and the chocolate bar and the peanut butter would wind up together.

Of course, then came the great debate: "You got your peanut butter on my chocolate." "No, you got your chocolate in my peanut butter." At this point, each of them would eat their chocolaty peanut butter (or peanut buttery chocolate) and simultaneously exclaim, "This is great!" It's fair to say that for the pair in the commercial, as well as for many who watched, the Reese's peanut butter cup indeed embodied the best of both worlds.

Remember how I mentioned at the end of the last chapter that human beings are body-persons? We have a soul with an intellect and will, so we belong to the spiritual world, *and* we have a body with all its senses, so we belong to the material world. Well, when you think about it, that means that human beings are the "*best* of both worlds."

So, what does this have to do with the Theology of the Body and with Jesus taking us back to "the beginning"? Actually, it has everything to do with it! In fact, it's the next lesson Jesus teaches us in *The Cosmic Prequel.* The second passage that Jesus alludes to in his answer to the Pharisees is the creation story of Genesis 2 (the Book of Genesis has *two* creation stories). Even though Genesis 1 states that God created human beings "male and female," Genesis 2 gives us the specifics of *how* and *why* he did so. The passage begins with the creation of the first man, Adam, from the dust or clay of the ground. Although Adam gets his name from the stuff he is made of (*adamah* is the

For Your Consideration

None of this means that these opening passages of the Bible must be taken "literally" as exact descriptions of historical events. That's not even how the people who wrote them understood them. These passages use mythical figures and images to describe primordial events and truths about God, us, and the world.

Hebrew word for "earth"), this doesn't mean that men are dirt. After God creates Adam from the clay of the ground, he breathes into him "the breath of life," and Adam becomes a "living being." The Hebrew word for "breath," *ruah,* is the same word for "spirit." So, the breath of life indicates that human beings are both physical *and* spiritual beings. In other words, they are *body-persons*. The sad reality is, however, that many people do not know this important truth.

Different Views of the Body

There's one school of thought that holds that a person is really identified with the soul, not the body. In other words, the soul is the real you. The body dies, after all, and the soul goes to heaven (or that other place). In this view the body is like a prison of the soul and is always making us do bad things. You could classify these ideas as being "down" on the body.

Another view holds that the soul does not exist at all, that we are just matter, and that when we're dead, we're dead. Life is merely about gaining pleasure and avoiding pain. "Eat, drink, and be merry, for tomorrow we die" sums up this creed.

Both of these views are flawed. Catholicism holds that human beings are both body and soul, not more one than the other. The fact that we die and our souls separate from our bodies is not part of God's original plan for us. Though death is natural for beings with bodies, in "the beginning" God gave human beings the gift of immortality so that their bodies took on the immortal quality of their souls. They kept this gift as long as their souls cleaved to God. So, you could say that God would "hold them together" as long as they "held onto him." For human beings, therefore, death is a consequence of original sin (more on that later).

Proofs of the Goodness of the Body

Jesus himself gives us proof positive of the goodness of the body as an essential part of human beings. If the body were bad, the Son of God would have never become enfleshed, and he certainly would not have taken his body back after he died. Not only that, Jesus ascended into heaven body and soul. And check this one out: after his resurrection he even ate (see Jn 21:12–14)! If that wasn't enough, the Blessed Virgin Mary was assumed into heaven body and soul. After she died, God took her right up!

Catholics believe in what we call "the resurrection of the body": at the end of time, we will all get our bodies back. They will be new and different from the ones we have now—what the Scriptures refer to as "spiritual bodies." We will go to heaven (or that other place) with our body and our soul, for all eternity (see Jn 5:25–29). In heaven we will not have an "outer-body" experience, but a "body-soul" experience! We will not just feel peace and fulfillment in our souls, but also experience the most radical bodily pleasure ever imagined. I firmly believe that heaven will have the most incredible sunsets, beautifully scented flowers, rockin' music, awesome ski slopes, and "wickedly" competitive baseball games ever dreamed of. And of course, my family and friends will be there to enjoy it all with me. This is all pretty awesome news, unless, of course, you wind up going to that other place. I'll leave that to your imagination. Let's just say that it will be as wretched as heaven is beautiful.

Catholicism is also a deeply sensual religion. That is, it's totally into the senses. God said that the physical world is "very good" (Gen 1:31), and therefore the experiences of the body (including eating Reese's peanut butter cups) are also very good. Jesus himself loved good food and good drink and even wondered if people would call him a glutton and a drunkard for it (see Mt 11:18–19)! I'm sure I don't have to convince you that he obviously was neither.

In saying that Catholicism is sensual, I mean that it emphasizes that God comes to us through the physical world and through our seeing, smelling, hearing, tasting, and touching. Just think about the Bible: burning bushes, pillars of cloud and fire, Passover meals, etc. Of course, there's Jesus himself, the "image of the invisible God" (Col 1:15). He was *God made man*—talk about God coming to us through the physical world! Also, think about the sacraments that Jesus instituted as a way for us to reach out and touch the divine—water, oil, bread, wine, the spoken word, bodily actions. This is all pretty earthy stuff. That's because Jesus knew that we are body-persons, and that he needs to come to us through our senses.

The Body Reveals the Person

Now, just because we are equally body and soul doesn't mean that they are equal players. The soul is supposed to be "in charge of" or, in traditional language, "move" the body. And even *within* the soul there is a certain hierarchy or ordering of powers. The intellect is supposed to be in charge of or move the will. So, the way God originally intended us to work from "the beginning" is as follows: the intellect knows what is good, and the will, acting in and through the body, chooses that good. This means that the body and the soul stand or fall together.

Notable Quotable

"It is neither the spirit alone nor the body alone that loves: it is man, the person, a unified creature composed of body and soul, who loves. Only when both dimensions are truly united, does man attain his full stature."
—Pope Benedict XVI

It also means that the body *reveals* the person. It is in and through the body that the person, a being with an intellect and will, is made visible and is able to be perceived and experienced. And since all human beings are created to love as God loves and give themselves as gifts to one another (in a way similar to but not exactly like the way husbands and wives love each other), the human body has what John Paul II calls a "nuptial" or marital meaning. It is in and through the body that human beings give themselves freely, totally, faithfully, and fruitfully for each other's good.

John Paul II strongly believed that these truths are essential to understanding the meaning and purpose of our existence. Because the body reveals the person and has a nuptial meaning, human beings are not merely made in the image of God, but are *the physical image of God* in the world!

So, let's refine our earlier definition of human beings:

Human beings,
as body-persons created in the image of the Trinity,
are endowed with intellects and wills, so they can make
a free, total, faithful, and fruitful gift of themselves,
in and through their bodies, for each other's good,
and thus form a communion of persons
and be the physical image of God in the world.

Now we're getting somewhere.

JOHN PAUL II
In His Own Words

The human body...includes right from the beginning the nuptial attribute, that is, the capacity of expressing love, that love in which the person becomes a gift and—by means of this gift—fulfills the meaning of his being and existence.

(*GA*, 1/16/80)

Things to Ponder and Share

1. What are some ways in which people can "undervalue" the body? "Overvalue" the body?

2. Define *adamah* and *ruah*. What do they reveal to us about man?

3. From your experience of church, give some examples of how Catholicism is "into" the senses.

4. What does it mean that the body "reveals the person" and has a "nuptial meaning"? Why are these truths essential to understanding the meaning and purpose of our existence?

5. How should the fact that "the body reveals the person" affect the way we treat our body or other people's bodies? Give some concrete examples.

6. Give some examples of the body's "nuptial meaning" in action.

Read the
Catechism of the Catholic Church

nos. 362–368, 1015–1017, 1146

CHAPTER 5

Lessons in Loneliness

Then the LORD God said, "It is not good that the man should be alone; I will make him a helper fit for him." So out of the ground the LORD God formed every beast of the field and every bird of the air, and brought them to the man to see what he would call them; and whatever the man called every living creature, that was its name. The man gave names to all cattle, and to the birds of the air, and to every beast of the field; but for the man there was not found a helper fit for him.

— Genesis 2:18–20

Why God Made Adam "Alone"

While I'm not that bad at math in general, algebra was definitely not my subject. No matter how many different ways my teacher explained things, I just didn't get it. So on those occasions when I felt particularly lost, I would seek out the help of a tutor. The intense, individual attention really helped me to fully and properly understand the lessons being taught to me. I am convinced that without it, I'd still be in tenth-grade math.

As a body-person, Adam in the above passage from Genesis has been made to love as God loves: to give himself freely, totally, faithfully, and fruitfully for the good of another through his body. No other creature has been made this way, and Adam knows it. But there's one small problem...there is no "other" to love. At least, not yet. For the time being, God wants Adam to be alone. God needs to teach him some important lessons, and unless Adam is alone, he won't fully and properly understand them. You could say that God schedules some one-on-one tutoring in order to guarantee "educational success."

The First Lesson:
Besides God There Is No Other

Now, your first thought may be: "But isn't there God? Isn't he an 'other'? Isn't he the 'ultimate other'?" That makes an excellent point! In fact, it's the first reason why God made Adam with no "other" to love. He wanted Adam to realize that besides him *there is no other. He* had to be first in Adam's life.

God is the *Alpha* and *Omega* (Rev 1:8), the beginning and the end—and everything in between. We owe our life and all that's in it to him. He made us, after all; we belong to him and, as a result, we should love him above all things. He is everything, and without him we would be nothing. This is the first lesson that God wants to teach Adam in his "loneliness." Adam has more lessons to learn, however.

The Second Lesson:
Love Requires Knowing What Is Good

God wanted to make it absolutely clear to Adam that love means freely giving himself for *the good* of another, so he decided it was time to teach Adam about what is good and what is evil. Remember the tree? The one that Adam couldn't eat from without dying? God had a good reason to call it the tree of the knowledge of good and evil. When God forbids Adam from eating of the fruit of this tree, lesson number two begins.

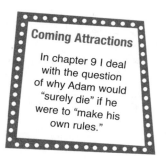

Coming Attractions

In chapter 9 I deal with the question of why Adam would "surely die" if he were to "make his own rules."

Look at the tree in this way: "not eating of the tree" means "choosing what God decides is good and not choosing what God decides is evil." On the other hand, "eating of the tree" means "deciding for yourself what is good and what is evil." Sound familiar? It is the quintessential clash within our culture and within ourselves: absolute truth vs. moral relativism, God's way vs. our way.

Moral relativism states that moral truth is *relative* to the individual: "Whatever you think is right and wrong *is* right and wrong." On the contrary, absolute truth means that moral truth is objective and universal: "There is a right and wrong, and it is right and wrong always, everywhere, and for every-body." In a way, every human choice places us at the tree. We always face the same temptation. Will we play by God's rules or try to make our own? Or will we even acknowledge that any rules exist at all?

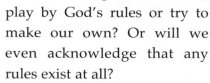

Notable Quotable

"With this imagery [of the Tree of the Knowledge of Good and Evil], Revelation teaches that *the power to decide what is good and what is evil does not belong to man, but to God alone...* God, who alone is good, knows perfectly what is good for man, and by virtue of his very love proposes this good to man in the commandments."
— Pope John Paul II

If Adam is going to be an "image of God" and "love as God loves," then he needs to know *the truth* about *what is good*. You can't have love without truth. This is what many people today have sadly missed: if there is no absolute truth, there is no true love either. This delusion also afflicts those who think they can love God and their neighbor, yet disregard the commandments. God's lesson to Adam is simple: If you are going to love, you must obey me.

The Third Lesson: Persons Are Different from Animals

Next, God wanted Adam to really experience in the depths of his being that he was "alone" in the world; that he alone was a person capable of giving himself to another. Why would God want such a thing? Because it was the most powerful way for Adam to realize the purpose of his existence. When

God declared, "It is not good that the man should be alone; I will make him a helper fit for him" (Gen 2:18), you can just imagine Adam's anticipation. Then, when the big moment finally arrived, the helper God created was...Eve, did you say? Nope. Actually, it was a cow. What a letdown!

Now, if you want to get technical, the Bible mentions both cows and birds by name, and then just states "and every beast of the field." But you must admit, God wasn't looking so bright just then. What was he doing? A *cow?* A *bird?* I mean, he has an omniscient reputation to live up to. You can almost see Adam's face saying, "You're kidding, right?"

Just a little tidbit: whenever God looks "dumb" in the Scriptures, it's obviously not that he *is* dumb, but that he's *playing* dumb. Why would he be playing dumb? Because God is a master teacher. Teachers typically ask their students loads of questions that they already know the answers to. They do so because students learn better by coming to the answers themselves. Teachers play dumb; students get smart. That's what God was doing here.

So what was God teaching Adam in this final "lesson in loneliness"? Simply put: *you are not an animal.* It's like God was saying, "Animals have bodies, but they aren't body-persons like you are. Animals know some things, but they don't know what is true, good, and beautiful like you do. Animals make some choices, but they're based on instinct or training, not on free choice like yours are.

Animals may form an attachment to you and you may really care for them, but you can't love each other—at least not the way I love my Son or I love you. Let's face it, Adam, you can't form a communion of persons with a cow or a bird. No, you need an 'other' like yourself, whom you can love in and through your body!"

Let's just say that Adam got the point. The more creatures he saw, the more alone he felt. Adam longed in the depths of his being for another whom he could love. Through the divine pedagogy—God's strategy—it became extremely clear to him that he would only find happiness and fulfill the purpose of existence by giving himself away to someone "just like him." This was Adam's deepest desire, and just when he thought all was lost, God met that desire...and then some.

JOHN PAUL II
In His Own Words

When God-Yahweh said, "It is not good that man should be alone" (Genesis 2:18), he affirmed that "alone," man does not completely realize this essence [of being a person]. He realizes it only by existing "with someone"—and even more deeply and completely, by existing "for someone."

(*GA*, 1/9/80)

Things to Ponder and Share

1. Some of life's most memorable lessons are
    learned one-on-one. Recall a time in your life
    when a parent, a relative, a teacher, a coach, or
    some other caring adult or good friend pulled
    you aside and imparted wisdom to you.

2. List and explain the three lessons God
    taught Adam.

3. Have you ever put other people or things
    before God in your life? If so, when?

4. Why is obedience to God's commandments
    necessary in order to love?

5. Name a time in your life when you "made your
    own rules" instead of obeying God's rules.
    What were the results/consequences of that
    decision?

6. Define moral relativism. Give some exam-
    ples of how moral relativism has become
    prevalent in our society.

7. How are humans quite different from animals?

Read the ——————————————
Catechism of the Catholic Church

nos. 144, 299–301, 338, 342–343,
1955, 2465   ◄—————————————

CHAPTER 6

A Match Made in Heaven

So the LORD God caused a deep sleep to fall upon the man, and while he slept took one of his ribs and closed up its place with flesh; and the rib which the LORD God had taken from the man he made into a woman and brought her to the man. Then the man said, "This at last is bone of my bones and flesh of my flesh; she shall be called Woman, because she was taken out of Man." Therefore a man leaves his father and his mother and cleaves to his wife, and they become one flesh. And the man and his wife were both naked, and were not ashamed.

— Genesis 2:21–25

The Creation of Eve and the First Married Couple

It's nearly impossible to listen to the radio, watch TV, or surf the Web without being barraged by ads for some "matchmaker" service. There are countless companies out there trying to convince people that they have the fool-proof system for finding their "perfect match" and the man or woman of their dreams. Well, the Book of Genesis dramatically reveals that God is the "Supreme Matchmaker" and *the One who will make our dreams of real love come true!*

God puts Adam into a deep sleep, takes one of his ribs, and creates the helper of his dreams. Talk about a match made in heaven! When Adam awakes, you could hear his delight a mile away. "Wow!" he exclaims. "She's beautiful. She's perfect. She's my equal. She's just like me...but different in all the right ways! We go together! We belong together! At last, one whom I can love in and through my body; one for whom I can give my life!" I truly believe that this is the gist of the whole "bone of my bones and flesh of my flesh" thing.

You see, God didn't really make Eve "just like" Adam. He made her a person like Adam, but he made her very different from Adam. God made Eve *complementary* to Adam. We know this because she was made to be his "helper." God knew all along that he was going to make them *to be each other's helpers.*

Think about when you typically ask for help. Isn't it usually when you can't do something? A helper is someone who makes up for what you lack. A helper is someone whose gifts complement your own. When people help each other, they are more than they are individually.

This is why God made human beings male and female. He made man with "a guy way of thinking, being, and acting" called *masculinity*, and he made woman with "a girl way of thinking, being, and acting" called *femininity*. Masculinity and femininity are harmonious. Man and woman are equal in dignity because they are both persons made in the image of God. But God created them with different gifts and different roles so that their union would be melodious rather than monotone, a symphony rather than a solo. I don't know about you, but it's music to my ears!

Giving the Body, Giving the Self

Adam and Eve found their "original happiness" in being each other's helper—in giving themselves totally and exclusively to one another in love. Adam looked at Eve and said, "Eve, I'm yours. I belong to you. I give myself freely, totally, faithfully, and fruitfully to you, and I will spend my life for your good." Eve accepted Adam's gift and returned it with a gift of her own: "And I, Adam, am yours. I belong to you. I give myself freely, totally, faithfully, and fruitfully to you, and I will spend my life for your good."

Notable Quotable

"Marriage based on exclusive and definitive love becomes the icon of the relationship between God and his people and vice versa. God's way of loving becomes the measure of human love."
— Pope Benedict XVI

God blesses their vows, and then they do with their bodies what their words said—they become

"one flesh" in sexual union. As the physical manifestation of their promises, the first human couple's
body language speaks the truth: "This is my body,
indeed my very self, given for you." The result is
some of the most mind-blowing bodily and spiritual pleasure ever imagined this side of eternity!

As Adam and Eve become one flesh through
their sexual union, God binds them together in love
with *His own love:* the Holy Spirit! This is why, as
Jesus reminds the Pharisees, "what God has joined
no human being must separate" or *can* separate. No
one can divide what God has united! Just as the Holy
Spirit unites the Father and the Son,
and they can never be separated
from one another, the Holy Spirit
unites the husband and wife, and
they can never be separated from
one another. This is the *original
unity* of man and woman as God
intended it from "the beginning."
And notice how Jesus said *"no
human being* must separate." Adam
and Eve's persons, indeed their lives,
have been fused together, and *not even they* can do
anything to change it. What's done is done.

> **Did U Know**
> The Holy Spirit also
> unites Christ and the
> Church. As St. Augustine
> said, Christ can never
> be "divorced" from the
> Church, which, by the
> way, has as one of
> its titles "Bride of Christ."

The second creation story of Genesis ends with:
"And the man and his wife were both naked, and
were not ashamed." Some people think that Adam
and Eve were never really married. This verse makes

it clear that they were. After their exchange of vows, blessed and approved by God, and their becoming one flesh in sexual union, they are fully pronounced *man and wife*. This is because, as we've already seen, their sexual union ratifies their vows, and the Holy Spirit binds them in an indissoluble unity.

The Naked Truth

This verse brings to our attention another very "revealing" topic: *nakedness*. Why did God inspire the biblical author to note that Adam and Eve were "naked and not ashamed"? It seems that there are two reasons, and both tell us something about the human body and the way we look at it. First, Adam and Eve were not ashamed of their nakedness because when they saw each other's bodies, they saw each other's *persons*. They recognized quite naturally that the body reveals the person. They didn't just see bodies. Just seeing bodies is the root of lust. The reduction of persons to their bodies actually depersonalizes them. It treats them like animals. They become nothing more than objects to be used according to another's good pleasure, certainly not persons to be loved for their own sakes.

Notable Quotable

"The Church continues to teach the unchanging truth that marriage is indissoluble. When couples freely receive this Sacrament [of Matrimony], they establish an unbreakable oneness. Their love for one another, their conjugal love, can last until death, not because of their own strength or merits but because of Christ's grace at work within them."
—Pope John Paul II

Because they were inclined to *perceive the person,* Adam's "love handles" and the extra pounds around Eve's hips didn't embarrass them or make them ashamed. Our contemporary culture, with its obsession with "hard bodies," has tragically missed this point. When Adam and Eve looked upon each other, all they saw was the most beautiful *person* in the entire world!

In order to understand the second reason why Adam and Eve were not ashamed of their nakedness, we need to interpret nakedness in a broader sense. To be naked can mean to be "exposed" or "vulnerable," "baring all" so to speak. Adam and Eve were completely open with each other, sharing everything: their thoughts, feelings, hopes, dreams, and fears. They allowed themselves to be vulnerable with each other. This took profound trust—but they felt safe. They knew they were completely focused on each other's good, so they had no fear of being used or manipulated by the other.

It was only after sin came on the scene that they needed to "cover up." Only then did they need to protect their bodies from the lustful gaze of the other. Only then did they need to protect their hearts from being broken by use, manipulation, dishonesty, and betrayal.

For now, however, they had found marital bliss. They had finally "met their match."

JOHN PAUL II
In His Own Words

The man [Adam] manifests for the first time joy and even exaltation, for which he had no reason before, owing to the lack of a being like himself. Joy in the other human being, in the second "self," dominates the words spoken by the man on seeing the woman. All this helps to establish the full meaning of original unity.

(GA, 11/7/79)

Things to Ponder and Share

1. Have you ever dreamed about your future spouse, your "match made in heaven"? What are his or her personal qualities? Why would he or she be your perfect match?

2. What are the different ways in which men and women are complementary? How have some aspects of society tried to downplay or even deny these God-given differences?

3. Give examples of how being a "helper" and giving oneself to another in love is the key to happiness.

4. How do the marriage vows (e.g., "for better or worse," etc.) express the meaning of life and

human existence (i.e., "to love as God loves")?
Why is marriage necessarily "until death do us
part"? Why does sexual union only "speak the
truth" after the marriage vows have been
exchanged?

5. What are the two reasons that God inspired
    the biblical author to note that Adam and Eve
    were "naked and not ashamed"?

6. Give examples of how our society often fails to
    "perceive the person" revealed in his or her
    body and instead sees humans as "just bodies."

Read the
Catechism of the Catholic Church

nos. 371, 373, 1605,
2333–2335

CHAPTER 7

God Is Pro-Life!

> God blessed them, and God said to them, "Be fruitful and multiply, and fill the earth and subdue it."
>
> — Genesis 1:28

The Call to Fruitfulness in Marriage

There's an old rhyme that goes: "First comes love, then comes marriage, then comes baby in a baby carriage." Though in reality it doesn't always happen this way, this simple phrase illustrates a fundamental truth about human love and human sexuality.

Fertility was the original blessing that the Creator bestowed upon the first married couple, and, as we'll see, it has everything to do with the "two becoming one flesh" and being made in the image of the Trinity. But it was also a *divine mandate.* Notice that the sentence "be fruitful and multiply" is an *imperative:* it gives a command, not a suggestion.

57

God did not say, "Be fruitful and multiply, unless you don't want to or it cramps your lifestyle." He also didn't say, "Be fruitful and multiply, unless it gets in the way of your other priorities." But he *did* say, "Be fruitful and multiply; fill the earth and subdue it." (My wife and I already have six children with plenty of child-bearing years to go, so you can see we take this verse very seriously!)

Now, God did not say that the man and his wife had to have sex twenty-four hours a day, seven days a week—after all, they had a garden to care for and cultivate (see Gen 2:15). He also didn't say that they had to have as many children as was "humanly conceivable." But it is clear that being fruitful and multiplying, and doing so generously, wasn't optional in God's original plan for marriage. And this generosity toward life was to be a *source of blessing* for the married couple and their children!

Marriage: A Life-Giving Communion of Persons

So, *why* would God command fruitfulness? And *how* could God command fruitfulness? Let's answer the first question first.

We have already shown that man and woman are persons who are made to love as God loves, in and through their bodies. We have also shown that God's love is a fruitful love, which is so radically inclusive that it always seeks to give life and is never intentionally sterile. When man and woman love as God loves, in and through their bodies, they form a communion of persons; they become completely one with each other or "one flesh." They most fully realize this one flesh communion of persons when, through their sexual union, the twenty-three chromosomes of the man become one with the twenty-three chromosomes of the woman. The child is the crowning event of the communion of the spouses. In a sense, the child completes the couple. You could even say that the child is the love of the spouses made a person—made a *third* person. When I look at my children running around my house, giggling and tearing it apart, I see the love of my wife and me *personified.*

Human beings are made in the image of the Trinity. The Trinity is a communion of persons— *three* persons. The love of the Father and the Son actually is the third Person in the family of the Trinity, whom we call the Holy Spirit. The Trinity is indeed the first family and the model family. Every human family is its image in the world.

Why then doesn't every family only have one child and be a "little trinity"? Because as limited beings who live in time, human beings can never express and communicate their persons perfectly or definitively. No one child can totally personify the love of a husband and wife. In fact, their love can never be totally personified—even if they had fifty children! But God's love can, for he is an all-perfect being who lives in eternity. The love between the

Father and the Son is perfectly expressed and communicated once and for all in the Holy Spirit. Nothing more can be added—God loves definitively in the third Person. Anything else would be redundant. However, the love among the divine Persons in the Trinity is not "self-contained." It continues creating: the universe, the earth, and you and I exist because of God's love.

Generosity Toward Life and Its Blessings

Just as God's love is creative, the love of the spouses, as the image of God's love in the world, should always be willing to include others in it and to give life to others. It, like God's love, should never be made intentionally sterile. The prevailing attitude between the spouses ought to be one of generosity toward new life, that there is always enough love to go around, and "the more, the merrier," so to speak.

Also, with more children, both parents and children have *more* opportunities to love. Let's face it, larger families have fewer options. If everyone and everything is going to be taken care of, everybody must do his or her part. In a sense, each family member must "take it for the team." The older members tend to the younger ones, the more able to the less able, and the healthy to the sick. Actually, in my family each older child is assigned as the helper for a younger child and assists them in brushing their teeth, getting them dressed, making their beds, and the like. And just as with a team, in the end everybody wins. The spouses not only give themselves totally to each other for one another's own good, but together they give themselves totally to their children for their children's own good. In turn, the children give themselves for each other's good, as well as for the good of their parents. As a result, every member of the family learns "to love as God loves" more perfectly with each passing day. This is why Mother Teresa used to say, "Love begins at home," and why Pope John Paul II was fond of calling the family a "school of love." And since we only "find ourselves" and our happiness in the "sincere gift of ourselves" (that is, in loving as God loves), you could also call the family a "school of happiness." Everyone gives, everyone receives, and everyone is blessed.

God Is the Lord of Life

That should answer *why* God commands fruitfulness; now let's look at the *how*. God can command it because he is the one in charge of it. When Eve gives birth to her firstborn son, she exclaims, "I have gotten a man with the help of the LORD" (Gen 4:1). God is the sovereign Lord of life. The Holy Spirit is the "Lord and Giver of life." Man and woman are called to cooperate in God's creating, and not to do anything deliberately to stop it. That's why we say God creates, but humans pro-create. God commands man and woman to be "pro" or "in favor of" his creating when he wills it and to place no obstacle in the way of it. Make no mistake about it: God is pro-life!

It's important to make clear that a couple that is *naturally* infertile, who through no deliberate choice is physically unable to bear children, do not have "less" of a marriage than a couple who has been blessed with many children. Neither is this couple "cursed" by God or "judged" by him as not deserving of children. Disabilities and disorders in nature are part of life in a fallen world. Couples who desire children of their own, yet cannot conceive them, suffer tremendously. Although such a couple *may use only morally acceptable means* available to them to relieve this burden, the Church certainly supports and encourages adoption. Adopting children can help their love to grow in perfection as they include others in it, and allow them to more fully share in the Creator's original blessing.

> **Notable Quotable**
>
> "...Even when procreation is not possible, [marital] life does not for this reason lose its value. Physical sterility...can be for spouses the occasion for other important services..., for example, adoption, various forms of educational work, and assistance to other families and to poor or handicapped children."
> — Pope John Paul II

Did U Know

While the Church strongly opposes reproductive technologies that "replace" the sexual union of spouses and "make" children in a laboratory (see chapter 16), she champions scientific advances that respect and protect the dignity of the human person and the marital act. For information on how science helps couples to conceive children naturally, visit www.popepaulvi.com.

Well, as we have seen, that original blessing means that God is pro-life. However, as Adam and Eve are about to learn, "The wages of sin is death" (Rom 6:23), not life.

JOHN PAUL II
In His Own Words

Procreation brings it about that the man and the woman (his wife) know each other reciprocally [together] in the "third," sprung from them both.... In a way it is a revelation of the new man, in whom both of them, man and woman, again recognize themselves.

(*GA*, 3/12/80)

Things to Ponder and Share

1. What are some ways in which people mistakenly view children as a burden rather than a blessing (e.g., as an impediment to a career, etc.)?

2. How does the family reflect the Holy Trinity?

3. Why would the Church support and encourage adoption, especially for naturally infertile couples?

4. How does the family help us to "love as God loves" every day? What are some families you know that are truly "schools of love"?

5. How is fruitfulness in marriage a blessing to both parents and children?

6. God is the sovereign Lord of life. What are some ways in which that is not acknowledged in our world today?

Read the
Catechism of the Catholic Church

nos. 372, 1604, 1652–1654

CHAPTER 8

Gone Fishing

Now the serpent was more subtle than any other
wild creature that the LORD God had made. He
said to the woman, "Did God say, 'You shall not
eat of any tree of the garden'?" And the woman
said to the serpent, "We may eat of the fruit of the
trees of the garden; but God said, 'You shall not eat
of the fruit of the tree which is in the midst of the
garden, neither shall you touch it, lest you die.'"
But the serpent said to the woman, "You will not
die. For God knows that when you eat of it your
eyes will be opened, and you will be like God,
knowing good and evil."

— Genesis 3:1–5

The Fall of the First
Man and Woman

I'm not a fisherman, but I went fishing once. A
friend of mine was moving from New Jersey to
Indiana, and he insisted on taking me fishing before
he left. So we planned to go one morning. When I
showed up at his house in the wee small hours, he
was all ready to go (he had even bought me my very
own fishing pole). We drove to his favorite fishing
hole, and he gave me a "crash course."

It turns out you need to know a few very important things to catch a fish. First, you've got to go where the fish are, that is, you've got to choose a good fishing hole. Second, you have to be as quiet and crafty as possible, so you don't scare the fish away. Third, you've got to choose the right bait: one that looks "good" or "harmless" to the fish, and can capture the fish's curiosity without alerting it to the danger. Finally, you need to cast a long line and reel it in slowly, so it looks natural and unassuming.

Check It Out

The serpent/Satan turns up again at the end of the Scriptures. See Revelation 12:9.

Well, Satan, who is symbolically represented in Genesis 3 by the serpent, knows a thing or two about fishing. Adam and Eve...well, they're the fish. And, actually, so are we.

Try to imagine the scene. Still basking in the afterglow of marital bliss, Eve decides to go out for some breakfast. Adam follows, and the two of them stroll into the garden. It is a beautiful morning: the sun is shining on their faces, the birds are chirping, and a gentle breeze is blowing across the lightly dew-laden grass. The man and his wife sense within their souls the union they had formed with each other. They feel it really and truly—down to the core. They also feel a profound oneness with the world around them. Joy, peace, and harmony rule creation. You could say it is "heaven on earth."

They are so caught up in the moment that they don't even realize they have meandered right into the middle of the garden. Then they see it: the tree. The serpent is already waiting. The tree is the "perfect fishing hole," and its fruit—the promise of *absolute freedom and independence*—the "perfect bait." Here Satan can try to get Adam and Eve to unlearn the lessons God had taught Adam in his loneliness: that they need God's rules in order to love and be truly happy, that besides God there is "no other," and that they are different from the animals. The serpent is ready to "cast a long line" in order to "hook" Adam and Eve. But he can't be obvious, lest he scare them away. He needs to be "subtle."

Satan the "Spin Doctor"

In this case, to be subtle means to be crafty or cunning; to be a master of fine distinctions. It means being able to take words and give them a little twist, practically undetectable yet enough to affect their meaning. It essentially means being a "spin doctor." In Satan's case, it means being particularly adept at *making what's good look like it's evil, and what's evil look like it's good,* in order to get us to believe that God didn't really mean what he said, or that somehow there's an exception for us.

Here's a modern example of Satan whispering subtleties in our ears:

"You love each other, right? Then go ahead and have sex! Sex is about love after all. It's a way to show your

love. And God is love, and even commands us to love, doesn't he? So how could sex be wrong?"

When you think about it, it's *technically true* that God is love and commands us to love, and that sex is about expressing love. But love cannot be achieved apart from what God has said is good, that is, apart from his commandments. That's where we see the almost undetectable twist I spoke of.

With this in mind, check out the first thing the serpent says to Eve: "Did God say, 'You shall not eat of *any* tree of the garden'?" Interestingly, the King James Version of the Bible uses the word "every" instead of "any." I believe this word better illustrates Satan's subtlety and intention here. Think about it: did God say that Adam and Eve couldn't eat of *every* tree in the garden? It turns out that indeed he did. God said that Adam and Eve could eat from *every tree but one,* and that means they can't eat from *every* tree. Enter the "spin zone."

Focusing on the Negative

The serpent knows full well that God had forbidden Adam and Eve from eating of the tree of the knowledge of good and evil. But the serpent *intends to make them think that they can achieve love and happiness apart from God's law, and that if they could only make their own rules, then they would be truly happy.* Eve responds just the way we would expect (and the way we all probably would have responded): "We may eat of the fruit of the trees of the garden; but

God said, 'You shall not eat of the fruit of the tree which is in the midst of the garden, neither shall you touch it, lest you die.'"

At first glance, it might seem as though Adam and Eve merely perceive a mistake on the part of the serpent, and Eve, speaking for them both, is simply correcting him. But her response also reveals that Satan's subtlety has begun to work on their thinking. How so? He has gotten Adam and Eve to become so focused on the one thing they *are not* allowed to do that they lose sight of all the things they *are* allowed to do. True, God had told Adam and Eve not to eat from the fruit of the tree or they would die. But if you go back to Genesis 2:15–17, you'll find *he never said a single thing about touching it!* Adam and Eve had become fixated on the one thing they couldn't do, and it seemed so oppressive to them that they made it even bigger than it was.

You may have fallen into this trap before. I think we all have. Our parents say "no" to something we really want to do, and we, not thinking of the freedom they do give us, blow it out of proportion and say something like, "You never let me do *anything.* You hate me. You're so strict. You don't want me to

> **Did U Know**
> Many think Eve was alone at the tree, but Adam was right there with her. Scripture makes this clear by adding: "she also gave some to her husband, who was with her..." The reason for this addition is that in the Bible's original language the serpent addresses the woman in the plural, as if he is speaking to *two* people.

have any fun. You want to ruin my life. I'm going, and there's nothing you can do to stop me." If we don't actually say these words, we think them. Well, that morning in the garden you could almost hear Adam and Eve's thoughts: "Gee, our Father in heaven is so strict. He never lets us do anything. We can't even touch that tree. He's completely unreasonable. Let's take it anyway—he can't stop us!"

Remember, every other tree in the garden was theirs for the picking—just not this tree. This tree was off limits, and God had only kept them from it because he loved Adam and Eve, wanted them to have a happy life, and knew that eating of the tree brought *danger* and meant certain death. This is hardly the work of an oppressive parent. So, the serpent knows that to "catch" Adam and Eve, he also needs to make them forget how much God loves them and wants them to be happy. He needs to get Adam and Eve to think that their heavenly Father doesn't really "know best," but that he, the serpent, is their "friend" and has the "inside scoop." In other words, he needs to inflict them with a little "parental amnesia," *so they will forget that God has given them everything, and that besides him there is no other.*

Forgetting the Father's Love

At some point in our lives we all suffer from "parental amnesia." We go from our parents being the ones who love us, keep us safe, and are the smartest and the strongest people in the world (you know, the whole "my dad can beat up your dad" thing) to our parents being the ones who don't know what they are talking about, are "out of touch," don't understand what we're going through, and want to keep us from making our own decisions. No longer feeling safe but smothered, we typically want our parents to just leave us alone (except when we need a ride or some money). Our friends then tend to take the place of our parents as the real authorities in life. This is usually when we begin to lose our "childhood innocence." We forget that our parents have seen a lot more of life than we or our friends have. We forget that there is probably no one in the world who loves us more than they, or want what's best for us, or want us to be happy, so we really can have confidence in their decisions (*confidence* comes from the Latin words *"con"* and *"fides,"* meaning "with faith or trust"). In my own case, my parents did wind up being right practically all the time, and I would have saved myself a lot of trouble if I hadn't "lost my memory."

Well, Satan wants Adam and Eve to lose their memory. He wants them to lose their innocence. He wants them to trust him as their friend and doubt God as their Father. The serpent's first approach: make it appear as though God doesn't know what he was talking about. "You will not die," the serpent said. Once again, *technically true.* Adam and Eve didn't eat the fruit and *physically* drop dead right then and there. Of course, they would eventually, but the serpent conveniently left that out. He also completely failed to mention the whole *spiritual death* thing that *would* happen then and there.

Satan's next move: get Adam and Eve to think that God really only cares about parental power, not love, that all he wants to do is spoil their fun and keep them from "growing up" and making their own choices. "God knows when you eat it you will be like him and can decide for yourself what's good and evil." In other words, "Grow up, be your own person, take a stand, take control of your life. What, are you going to let your Father make all your decisions for you?"

That's all Adam and Eve need to hear. They have the motivation, now all they need are the excuses. They see that the fruit is yummy, pretty, and intellectually stimulating, and they waste no time: they take some and eat it. At this point, Adam and Eve are primarily "thinking with their stomachs," that is, they are acting on their base instincts and drives. Hence, God's final lesson to Adam, *you are not an animal,* is undone as well. Animals by nature act on instincts and drives, but human beings don't. As persons endowed with intellects and wills, human beings can "think before they act." According to the story, it seems as if Adam and Eve don't really want to give themselves time to think about their decision, lest they "flounder."

But they sure did flounder: hook, line, and sinker, right onto the deck of the serpent's fishing boat! *Sin, suffering, and death had entered into human history.* "The beginning" had come to an end. Adam and Eve had lost their *original innocence,* and along with it, their chances for real love, true happiness, and a rich life.

JOHN PAUL II
In His Own Words

The man who gathers the fruit of the "tree of the knowledge of good and evil" makes, at the same time, a fundamental choice. He carries it out against the will of the Creator, God-Yahweh, accepting the motivation suggested by the tempter.... This motivation clearly includes questioning the gift and the love from which creation has its origin as donation [gift].

(*GA,* 4/30/80)

Things to Ponder and Share

1. How does Genesis 3 reveal that Satan knows a thing or two about fishing? What are the lessons he wants Adam and Eve (and us) to "unlearn"?

2. Why can subtlety be much more dangerous than it seems? Give examples of how subtlety can exist today.

3. Has there ever been a time in your life when you have been tempted to pursue happiness apart from God's law? If so, when? What resulted?

4. Have you ever focused so much on what you are not allowed to do that you forgot about all the things you are allowed to do? Explain the situation.

5. Have you ever suffered from "parental amnesia"? Give one example.

6. Name a time when you didn't "think before you acted." Why did you do so? What was your decision based on?

Read the
Catechism of the Catholic Church
nos. 386–387, 391–401

CHAPTER 9

The Great
Divorce

The LORD God then called to the man and asked him, "Where are you?" He answered, "I heard you in the garden; but I was afraid, because I was naked, so I hid myself."...[To the man God said:] "... you are dirt, and to dirt you shall return."

— Genesis 3:9–10, 19 NAB

The Effects of Original Sin on Humanity

My family has always loved baseball. My father made sure that I knew how to throw and catch a ball, as well as hit one pretty solidly, by the age of two. I'm not kidding—*two*. As I grew to play in an organized league, my parents began a family tradition. After one game each week we would go directly out to dinner, either at the local pizza joint or Burger King. There I'd be, dressed in a filthy clay-covered, grass-stained uniform and cleats, still sweating from the game, devouring my bacon double cheeseburger, fries, and a Coke at speeds rivaling the fastest Formula One car. It would have given the Board of Health nightmares. But for a ten-year-old kid, it was magic.

Burger King had reached the height of its popularity then, and they had a silly little jingle that was practically synonymous with the "home of the Whopper." It went something like this: "Have it YOUR way, HAVE it your way, have it YOUR way at Burger King.®" It was addictive. You couldn't get it out of your head. It's like a song they beat to death on the radio, but no matter how overplayed it is, and how much you cringe every time it comes on, later on you find yourself singing it anyway.

Well, if you think about it, God is like Burger King (and it's not just the *King* part). Though he wants us to do it his way, he lets us have it our way. God knows that just as love requires the truth about what is good, it also requires the freedom to choose it. He didn't tell Adam and Eve not to eat the fruit of the tree and then tie their hands behind their backs or put duct tape over their mouths. If he did, their choice "not to eat" wouldn't have been a choice at all. No choice, no love. It's as simple as that.

Choices Always Have Consequences

Like Adam and Eve's, our "yes" to God, which is also a "yes" to love, would mean nothing unless we could say "no." Ultimately, however, our choice will have a consequence. *Choices always have conse-*

quences. Some choices have *major consequences.* Adam and Eve's certainly did.

God respects our choices so much that he lets us live (and die) with them and their consequences—even if we wind up making a "whopper" of a mistake. *And Adam and Eve made a "whopper" of a mistake.* The famous British writer C. S. Lewis (who wrote *The Lion, the Witch, and the Wardrobe*) said that ultimately this world has two types of people: the ones *who say to God,* "Thy will be done," and the ones *to whom God says,* "Thy will be done." In other words, God says, "Have it YOUR way....®"

Check It Out

This statement is found in C.S. Lewis's charming book titled *The Great Divorce.*

Traditionally defined, sin is "an offense against God and his law." However, it can also be understood as *"a choice not to love* God with all of one's mind, heart, soul, and strength, and our neighbor as ourselves." By sin we turn away from "loving as God loves," and, therefore, turn away from the meaning of our existence and forfeit our personal happiness. If love means "communion," sin means "separation": separation from God, from others, and from our true selves.

The first earthly separation or "divorce," believe it or not, did not involve a man and a woman. It involved a man, a woman, and God. Adam and Eve divorced themselves from God. They ate from the fruit of the tree that God had forbidden. They chose to have absolute freedom and independence; to live for themselves and make their own rules. And God said, "Have it your way.®" He doesn't force them to love him, and so he lets his children walk away—even though he knows the trouble that's in store for them. It's the hardest thing a father has to do.

When Adam and Eve divorced themselves from God and committed the *original sin,* they left all their hopes for being "like God" behind. In a sense, the irony of the serpent's enticement—"you will be like God"—is that Adam and Eve already *were* like God. The serpent made it seem as if they needed to grasp at divine life, but they had already received it as a gift. Adam and Eve should have responded to the serpent by saying, "Sorry. Been there, done that." But they didn't. By choosing to eat the forbidden fruit in order to be like God, they actually became *unlike* him.

> **For Your Consideration**
>
> Contrast this attitude of our first parents with Jesus, the New Adam, who "though he was in the form of God, did not count equality with God a thing to be grasped..." (Phil 2:6).

Human Nature: "Out of Order"

When God created Adam and Eve, he endowed them with souls (having the powers of intellect and will) *and* bodies. Their intellects were supposed to know the good and direct their wills to choose it. Their souls would then direct their bodies toward right action. This "order" or *hierarchy* within a

human person would
exist as long as his or
her soul remained in
communion with God.

When they ate from
the fruit of the tree,
however, and rejected
God as their true Other
and the Lord of life,
their entire world began
to unravel like a thread
pulled from a sweater.
Divorced from God,
their very nature as
body-persons became
so *disordered* that loving
as God loves in and

through their bodies became virtually impossible.
The order that existed *within* their souls, as well as
the order that existed *between* their bodies and their
souls, was thrown into disarray. Satan, the first
rebel, had instigated Adam and Eve's rebellion
against God. Adam and Eve's rebellion in turn
caused an uprising or rebellion within their own
persons. Their intellects no longer submitted to
what was good. Their wills no longer obeyed their
intellects. And their bodies no longer followed the
directions of their souls. You could say that sin
turned everything "inside out and upside down,"
and caused human nature to be "out of order."

Adam's response to God after eating the fruit reveals this disorder: "I was afraid, because I was naked, so I hid myself." Adam's own words show that the relationship of his soul to his body had been damaged. In fact, because of original sin, human beings had now become "damaged goods." They were still fundamentally good since they were made by God, and a spark of God's original plan still flickered in them, but they had become "psychosomatically challenged." They wanted to know good and evil, but their intellects had become so confused that they lost much of their ability to know good and evil when they saw it. They wanted to make their own decisions, but their wills had become so weak that, even if their intellects knew what was good, they had lost much of their ability to choose it (see Rom 7:19, 22–23). They wanted to be free and "like God," but their souls had become such slaves to the instincts and drives of their bodies that they had become more like the animals. They wanted to "gain the whole world" and "lost their own souls," as well as Paradise, in the process.

Yet, this is the life they chose. *Human choices are self-determining,* which simply means that our choices make us who we are. There are two kinds of human dignity: the kind *God gives us* and we *already have* simply by virtue of being made in his image, and the kind we *give ourselves* and *achieve* by our free choices.[2] You may have heard the saying: "Sow an act, reap a habit. Sow a habit, reap a character. Sow a character, reap a destiny."[3] C. S. Lewis once said that by our choices we make ourselves into either a heavenly or hellish creature, and that when we die we simply go where we belong.[4] Humans are the only beings who can choose NOT to be what they were created to be. A tree can't choose not to be a tree; a dog can't choose not to be a dog; but a human can choose not to be human. A human being can choose not to be the "image and likeness of God" he or she was created to be from "the beginning." And the road to inhumanity starts with a single choice.

Death: The Ultimate Consequence of Sin

Now, besides being "out of order," another thing happened when Adam and Eve divorced themselves from God: they were "doomed to die," because God was their source of life. Their souls had separated from God, so one day they would also separate from their bodies—the ultimate insult to body-persons. Their bodies would "return to the dirt," and their souls would be consigned to a dismal eternal existence since they would be without God, who is their supreme good and ultimate happiness (or, as theologians would say, beatitude). Death is the natural consequence of sin. Believe it or not, it is also its appropriate punishment. As St. Paul said, "The wages of sin is death" (Rom 6:23).

Did you know that the seriousness of a crime is determined not only by "what is done" but by "to whom it is done"? Well, what if the person offended is God? That would make the crime *infinitely serious.* Since God is an infinite and eternal Person, the punishment would have to be infinite and eternal in order for it to fit the crime. That's where death comes in. The real bummer is that, since humans are finite beings, there's nothing they can ever do to "redeem themselves." Finite beings can never make up for an infinite offense. Not even the death of every human being who ever lived or will ever live, added together, could do that. No, humans would need a redeemer, a Savior. They would need someone who was human and could pay the debt on their behalf, but who also was infinite and could "afford" the debt they needed to pay. They would also need someone who could put the pieces of their human nature back together again. They would need the *King himself,* not just his horses and men. They would need the God-man. And God so desires for human beings to be reconciled to him, he so desires for human beings to fulfill the meaning and purpose of their existence and be happy, that he meets that need head-on!

But let's not get too far ahead of ourselves. We're not done with Genesis quite yet.

JOHN PAUL II
In His Own Words

The words, "I was afraid, because I was naked,"...show clearly the consequences in the human heart of the fruit of the tree of the knowledge of good and evil. Through these words a certain constitutive break within [the make up of] the human person is revealed, which is almost a rupture of man's original spiritual and somatic [bodily] unity.... The body is not subordinated to the spirit as in the state of original innocence. It bears within it a constant center of resistance to the spirit.

(*GA*, 5/28/80)

Things to Ponder and Share

1. Have you ever made a "whopper" of a mistake? What was it? What were the consequences?

2. Explain why our "yes" or "no" to our heavenly Father is simultaneously a "yes" or "no" to love.

3. How does sin "divorce" us from God, others, and our true selves?

4. Name a time when you knew the right thing to do but had a really hard time doing it.

5. Sometimes our bodies "tell" us to do something we know isn't good for us. When has this happened to you? How did you deal with it?

6. Give examples from history, society, or your personal experience of how our choices make us "who we are."

Read the
Catechism of the Catholic Church

nos. 402–405, 1707

CHAPTER 10

Fashion Statements

Then the eyes of both of them were opened, and they realized that they were naked; so they sewed fig leaves together and made loincloths for themselves. When they heard the sound of the LORD God moving about in the garden at the breezy time of the day, the man and his wife hid themselves from the LORD God among the trees of the garden.

— Genesis 3:7–8 NAB

The Entrance of Lust and Shame

"Beauty is in the eye of the beholder." "Don't judge a book by its cover." "Beauty isn't only skin deep." These are all variations on the same lesson we've heard a thousand times before. It's inspired countless works in literature, theater, and film, including the classic fable "Beauty and the Beast" by Madame Leprince de Beaumont, the literary masterpiece *Jane Eyre* by Charlotte Bronte, and *Shrek*, the irreverent animated film. Have you ever wondered, though,

why we constantly need to be reminded of this truth?

Well, after eating the fruit of the tree of the knowledge of good and evil, Adam and Eve began to have serious vision problems. I have always found it interesting that the biblical author chose the phrase: "Then the eyes of both of them were opened...." Their eyes may have been opened, but they definitely weren't seeing 20/20. In fact, they had become radically nearsighted. They couldn't see past themselves. Their sin had caused lust to fill their hearts, which in turn distorted their perception of the world and each other.

The man and woman who were *created for love* had become the man and woman who were *conquered by lust*. As such, Adam and Eve could no longer easily see each other as *body-persons* made in the image of God, "towards which the only proper and adequate attitude is love."[5] Instead, they were inclined to view each other as *simply bodies;* as objects to be used for their own purposes. They no longer readily beheld the beauty of each other's person, in fact, they *de-personalized* one another. Love says, "I *give myself* for *your* own sake." Lust says, "I *take you* for *my* own sake."

St. John says in his First Letter that lust has three components: there is the *lust of the eyes, the pride of life,* and the *lust of the flesh* (see 1 Jn 2:16–17). It's the "lust of the eyes" that moves us to see others as objects; to view one another as "just bodies" and not body-persons. The "pride of life" motivates us to act on this "vision" and to seek to "rule" over others and use them for our own selfish desires. The "lust of the flesh" directs these acts toward satisfying the desires of the body and gaining physical pleasure.

> **Check It Out**
>
> *Naked Without Shame* is the title of an audio CD series by Christopher West, an internationally renowned speaker and author of *Pope John Paul's Theology of the Body,* and is available from the GIFT Foundation.

Realizing they were infected by this threefold lust, Adam and Eve "sewed fig leaves together and made loincloths for themselves" (Gen 3:7). Before sin they were "naked without shame. After sin they were "naked and ashamed." But why?

Ashamed of Their Lust

Contrary to popular belief, Adam and Eve weren't ashamed of their bodies—they were ashamed of the lust that had crept into their hearts. They were ashamed because they knew it shouldn't be there, yet they couldn't get rid of it. Sin had "disabled" their nature. Adam no longer saw Eve's person; for him, her beauty was "only skin deep." She became just a body, an "object" he could use and dominate: "your husband...shall rule over you." He would exploit and manipulate her for his own pleasure, as in the classic line, "If you loved me, you would...." But he knew in the depths of his being that exploiting her was wrong. And he was ashamed.

Eve for her part used Adam. Eve learned pretty quickly how to get Adam to do what she wanted. She would *get* control by making him *lose* control. She would have her material and emotional needs met, and she would do whatever it took—*even allow herself to be used.* But she knew in the depths of her being that using him was wrong. And she was ashamed.

If you don't get what I am saying, imagine your typical school dance. What do you see? How do the guys look at the girls? How are the girls dressed and why? What does the atmosphere encourage? What does the dancing resemble? And what's it all for? Don't you think guys and girls leave those dances "ashamed," with their integrity knocked down a few pegs? I know I've seen my share of tears, quarrels, confusion, fear, and frustration.

The truth is that after the first sin even sex itself became dissatisfying. Though sex is still good (God created it, after all), lust keeps it from being every-thing God intended it to be from "the beginning." Sure, the drives are still there. The physical sensa-tion is still there. But the end result isn't joy. That's because the union of persons no longer seems accomplished in the union of bodies—and our hearts really long for the union of persons. Selfish motives—some conscious, some not—block total self-giving. The more this is the case, the shallower the "pleasure" and the more intense the shame. The biblical narrative indicates that, generally speaking, women are more "in touch" with and affected by this lack of communion, and yearn for something more: "your desire shall be for your husband...." This in no way means that guys aren't and don't; it's just less apparent in guys and they tend not to notice it as much. Guys tend to *replace* bodily union for personal union. Yet most guys still truly seek personal union, whether they realize it or not. *Girls confuse love for sex; guys confuse sex for love.* All too often, however, this confusion becomes a source of selfish manipulation: *Guys use love for sex; girls use sex for love.* And neither gets what they are look-ing for.

Do you remember when I said that men and women were created to *complement* each other? It should be obvious that after sin that *original comple-mentarity* became a *historical conflict.* "The begin-ning" ended, and the "battle of the sexes" began. We have seen the wars and witnessed the devastation:

from the oppression of women as little more than a
husband's property with no rights or place in the
public forum, to the form of radical
feminism that views women as
being the same as men (as opposed
to equal to men) and promotes contraception, abortion, lesbianism, and
having "babies without husbands."
Then, of course, there's divorce, the
breakdown of the family, illegitimacy,
sexually transmitted diseases, eating
disorders, loneliness, broken hearts,
scarred emotions, feelings of regret, and
feelings of worthlessness—I'm sure you
get the idea.

What else could Adam and Eve do but cover
up? It was the only way to protect themselves *from
themselves* and from each other. But, in a way, being
"clothed with shame" and being "clothed with fig
leaves" also reveal that Adam and Eve were still
"fashionable." They still had something to work
with. Adam and Eve had not lost God's original
plan entirely. A hint of it was left, an echo if you will.
They could still detect it; they could still hear it,
even though lust had clouded their vision and
clogged their ears. Neither the serpent nor their sin
had been able to drive God's original plan from
them fully. And they dressed accordingly.

In this way, shame has a positive effect: it
attempts to preserve the nuptial meaning of the

body. It helps us to see our bodies as the way in which we give ourselves to others and express love. It causes human beings to regard the body with the dignity it deserves, since the body reveals the person. In short, when we protect our bodies, we protect ourselves.

For this reason, the *virtue of modesty*—which "inspires one's choice of clothing" to guide "how one looks at others and behaves toward them"— doesn't have anything to do with the body being "dirty." It has everything to do with body-persons being beautiful images of God. Modesty protects the person. Modesty helps us to "perceive the person." By "wearing loincloths," we divert attention from our private parts and once again learn to "look into each other's eyes" and see into each other's souls. In the process, we not only protect ourselves from the lustful gaze of others, but we help others not to gaze lustfully. It's not love but lust that says, "If you've got it, flaunt it."

The Fear of Being Exposed

Now, fear almost always accompanies shame. The first thing Adam and Eve do after they "cover up" is "run for cover"—they bolt for the forest when they hear God approaching. When we are ashamed, we rarely want anybody else to discover what we're ashamed of. Adam and Eve didn't want each other to find out about the lust that had crept into their hearts. But that doesn't work with God. The

Scriptures say that God knows everything in our minds and hearts (see Ps 44:20–21, 139; Jn 2:25).

The Scriptures also say that "every one who does evil hates the light, and does not come to the light, lest his deeds should be exposed" (Jn 3:20). Well, "God is light." Even if we don't come to the light, eventually it will come to us. That is what happened with Adam and Eve. They knew that they had done evil and had disobeyed the God who created the universe and whose voice "flashes forth flames of fire" and "strips the forests bare" (Ps 29:7, 9). So, they ran from him. I don't think they ever imagined that he would search for them. "Where are you?" God asks (as if he didn't know). By the tone of God's voice, Adam and Eve know *he knows.*

Rather than "own up" and take responsibility, however, Adam and Eve try to avoid it. Shame almost always goes hand in hand with denial. Let's face it, we are very quick to take responsibility for the good things we do: good grades, sports accomplishments, success in the arts, good deeds to the poor, etc. We love to say, "Look what I did!" We never say something like, "I really can't take credit for that. I mean, my intelligence is genetic, my parents have instilled good discipline habits in me, and my teachers are masterful and have taught me great studying techniques." Conversely, however, *we are rarely willing to take responsibility for the bad things we do.* We usually find somebody to blame: "So and so told me to do it," or "I didn't know" (i.e., "No one told me"), or "Everybody else was doing it," or "The test was unfair—the teacher didn't cover the material," etc. It's funny, we say we want *absolute freedom and independence* with regard to our choices, when what we really want is absolute freedom from *the consequences* of our choices. But we can't have it both ways. If we're responsible for the good we do, then we're responsible for the bad as well.

The Blame Game

So, Adam and Eve go from *shame* to *blame*. God confronts Adam with his sin, and Adam blames Eve, and, implicitly, he also blames God: "That *woman* that *you* created made me do it. Some helper she turned out to be." God then confronts Eve, and she blames the serpent and, implicitly, both God and Adam: "The serpent tricked me. By the way, didn't *you* create him? And Adam, you were right there with me—why didn't you say something? Why didn't you do something to stop me?"

The blame game is a very big part of the battle of the sexes. It becomes very obvious when a couple gets divorced. The children are often caught in between and get the "low down" from each parent about everything that's wrong with the other. It's incredibly painful to watch, and even more painful to live. It's such a real-life drama that it has inspired many major motion pictures.

But the blame game is being played everywhere the battle of the sexes rages. To avoid responsibility for our actions with regard to sex, I have heard such attempts as, "When she dresses like that, how can I resist?" "But he told me he loves me." "Why did God give me these hormones, anyway?"

We've certainly come quite a distance from seeing each other as the "helpers" God fashioned us to be. And though we're ashamed of ourselves, there's still hope. Not all has been lost. God's original plan still echoes in our hearts.

JOHN PAUL II
In His Own Words

Lust...indicates an experience of value to the body, in which its nuptial meaning ceases to be that.... Its procreative meaning likewise ceases.... Man is ashamed of his body because of lust. In fact, he is ashamed not so much of his body as precisely of lust. He is ashamed of his body owing to lust.... It can even be said that man and woman, through shame, almost remain in the state of original innocence. They continually become aware of the nuptial meaning of the body and aim at preserving it from lust.

(*GA*, 9/10/80, 5/28/80, 6/25/80)

Things to Ponder and Share

1. What are some ways that beauty is not just "skin deep"? Does our society value them? Why or why not?

2. What are the three components of lust? Explain each and how they are related.

3. This chapter listed some examples of the devastation caused by the battle of the sexes. Would you add or subtract anything from this list? If so, why?

4. Do you think guys and girls manipulate one another to get what they want? If so, in what ways? Have you ever witnessed this in your own life or in the lives of those around you? If so, when?

5. What are some ways in which guys and girls can help one another "perceive the person" through practicing the virtue of modesty?

6. Have you ever played the blame game? When and why?

Read the
Catechism of the Catholic Church
nos. 369–370, 2521–2524

CHAPTER 11

Hearts Too Hard to Love

> They said to [Jesus], "Why then did Moses command one to give a certificate of divorce, and to put her away?" He said to them, "For your hardness of heart Moses allowed you to divorce your wives, but from the beginning it was not so."
>
> — Matthew 19:7–8

Why "the Beginning" Seems So out of Reach

Have you ever heard the saying, "Art mimics culture"? I don't know if it's true, but if it is, our culture often seems to convey the message: *sin is "in," and God's original plan is "out."*

Just take a look at the entertainment industry, for example. Now, don't get me wrong, there are certainly songs, movies, and TV shows out there that promote human and Christian values, and the media play a very important role in our society. But what are the messages being sent about life, love, marriage, and sex in much of what's considered "mainstream" today?

Now that we have looked at Satan's fishing technique, sin, and sin's devastating impact on human nature, we can easily understand why distorted messages are so prevalent and why we appear to be so far from God's original plan for life, love, marriage, and sex. Satan's subtlety is still at work in the world. If he can get you to hum the tune, laugh out loud, or make you root for the main characters to "hook up," then he's "hooked" *you.* Sometimes all Satan needs to do is desensitize us and get us to believe that sexual sin is "no big deal" and not all that harmful.

When we look around us, it may seem as though our world overvalues sex. No matter where you turn, it's "in your face," right? You just have to walk through your local shopping mall to be bombarded with the clothing or underwear displays. Or just walk through the grocery store check-out line and catch the gossip and fashion magazines: who's having an affair with whom in Hollywood or Washington and, of course, there's those scantily clad women and men and articles like "10 Tricks to Drive Your Man Crazy" and "All the New Great Sex Tips You'll Want to Know."

Actually, our world places *too little* value on sex. Think about it. Today sex often becomes primarily about seeking physical pleasure. For all intents and purposes, it's a recreational activity, like any other. There are videos to help you with your golf swing, and there are videos to help you to "spice up your sex life." People often judge each other mostly in terms of their sexual desirability. The sheer number of breast augmentation surgeries per year should prove that. According to the American Society for Aesthetic Plastic Surgery, the number of eighteen-year-olds who underwent breast-implant surgery nearly tripled from 2002 to 2003, and supposedly it has even become trendy for parents to give implants as a high school graduation gift. It has also become generally socially acceptable to commit practically any sort of sexual act with just about anyone, as long as everybody agrees. Things don't seem much different among teens. It appears that "hooking up" (a vague term that means everything from "making out" to oral sex) has become more common among teens than "going out" (dating).6 I recently heard that some teen and preteen girls even wear colored bracelets that secretly announce how far they are willing to go with a guy. Not much is taboo anymore.

> **For Your Consideration**
>
> This information comes from an article by Jeane MacIntosh cited in the *New York Post* online edition ("Cup and Gown," June 14, 2004). According to the article, experts believe that "popular, well-endowed teen idols... as well as reality-TV shows...have made some girls dislike their own bodies."

So our world isn't oversexed—it's *undersexed!* Just like Adam and Eve, people today miss the point of sex entirely. They miss what being created *male and female* is all about. They miss what being *body-persons* is all about. They miss what the *life-giving communion of persons* that God created a husband

and wife to express through their sexual union is all
about.

Hard Hearts, Rebellious Hearts

To return to Jesus' conversation with the Pharisees,
his response to their question wasn't directed only
to them. When Jesus said, "for your hardness of
heart Moses allowed you to divorce your wives...."
he meant your heart and my heart as well. Basically,
Jesus was saying that apart from God, *the human
heart has become too hard to love.*

In the Scriptures, the phrase "hardness of heart"
refers generally to a person's rebellion against God.
It also refers to the resulting *state of separation*—our
being "out of order." Therefore, "hardness of heart"
can be taken to refer to original sin and its negative
impact on our nature.

With this in mind, the meaning of Jesus' words
becomes clear. When Jesus said to the Pharisees,
"for your hardness of heart," he meant, "because of
sin." It's as if he were saying, "You were made in my
image, to love one another freely, totally, faithfully,
and fruitfully in and through your bodies. But sin
devastated your ability to do that. So, recognizing
your limitations, Moses allowed you to divorce
your wives."

I mentioned in the last chapter that God's original plan still echoes in the depths of our being. We
still aspire for true and lasting happiness. We still
desire to love and be loved. We still basically want

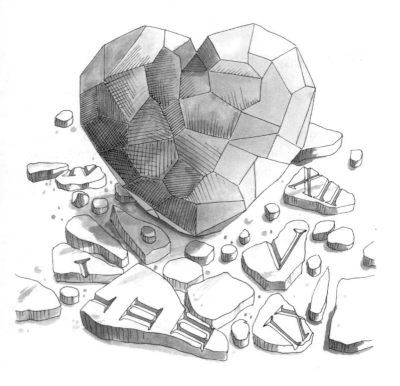

goodness and justice. We still search for God...
but now we are inclined to look for happiness in
temporary pleasures. Lust and uncontrolled emotions often impersonate real love. Selfish motives
and moral relativism corrupt goodness and justice.
And we tend to make God and religion into whatever suits our fancy or brings us comfort at the time.

Happiness Lost

All of this, of course, has a direct effect on both our
earthly and eternal happiness, since it contradicts
everything we were made for from "the beginning."
When you think about it, after original sin human
beings are really in quite a pathetic situation.

We started by saying:

1. To be happy, we need to be fully human.
2. To be fully human, we need to be the image
   and likeness of God we were created to be.
3. To be the image and likeness of God we
   were created to be, we need to love as God
   loves in and through our bodies.
4. Therefore, to be happy we need to love as
   God loves in and through our bodies.

But then we learned about the entrance of original sin and its effect on human nature.

1. Sin makes us it practically impossible for
   us to love as God loves in and through our
   bodies.

2. Therefore, sin makes it practically impossible for us to be the image and likeness of God we were created to be.
3. Therefore, sin makes it practically impossible for us to be fully human.
4. Therefore, sin makes it practically impossible for us to be happy.

In reaching for happiness apart from God and his law, Adam and Eve lost both their happiness and God. This is the paradox of sin: it promises fulfillment, but brings emptiness; it promises freedom, but brings slavery; it promises "heaven," but brings hell.

Even worse, original sin is not just an event—it's a condition. When Adam and Eve had children, they passed their damaged (sometimes called *fallen*) nature on to them, as well as the unhappiness that came with it. And there's none of that "skipping a generation" thing. Since we are technically all descendents of Adam and Eve, *all human beings* have the condition or disorder known as original sin. All, that is, except for the New Adam and the New Eve, who begin the new humanity that will live by new rules (which really aren't so much "new rules" as the "original rules" God had made from "the beginning").

Although God let human beings have it their way and suffer the consequences of sin in their lives, he never stopped caring for them. One of the first things God did after punishing Adam and Eve was make them better clothes—nice, new, leather ones (see Gen 3:21). And even in the midst of his punishments, God made humanity a promise. He promised that he would send a Savior to "strike at the head" of the serpent and redeem human beings from the power of sin and death (see Gen 3:15).

Did U Know
Theologians call this first prophecy of the Messiah in Genesis 3:15 the *proto-evangelium*, the first proclamation of the Gospel.

If sin and its devastating effects were the end of the story, we wouldn't call God's plan for us "Good News," would we? Humanity's got to make its comeback.

And indeed it does.

JOHN PAUL II
In His Own Words

[As a result of sin] the structure of communion between persons disappears. Both human beings become almost incapable of attaining the interior measure of heart, directed to the freedom of the giving of oneself and nuptial meaning of the body, which is intrinsic [essential] to it.

(*GA*, 7/30/80)

Things to Ponder and Share

1. What are some of the *subtle* and *not so subtle* messages out there today about life, love, marriage, and sex? Give specific media-related examples from advertisements, commercials, TV shows, movies, and music.

2. What are some ways in which sex seems to be everywhere you turn?

3. How does our society actually place *too little* rather than *too much* value on sex?

4. How has the human heart become too hard to love? What are some examples of this?

5. Outline the connection between our personal happiness and the need to love as God loves in and through our bodies. How does sin corrupt this?

6. Even with the apparently hopeless situation that sin has caused, why is there still reason to hope for the future?

Read the
Catechism of the Catholic Church

nos. 388, 407–412,
1608–1610, 2515

CHAPTER 12

The Divine Do-Over

Then as one man's trespass led to condemnation for all men, so one man's act of righteousness leads to acquittal and life for all men. For as by one man's disobedience many were made sinners, so by one man's obedience many will be made righteous.

— Romans 5:18–19

Jesus Christ Brings Us Back to "the Beginning"

As young boys attending grammar school, we looked forward to nothing more in our day than lunch recess. We would practically inhale our food so we could be the first out the door. At my school, lunch recess meant kickball. And let me tell you, we were pretty hardcore. We even kept stats. Inevitably, however, at least once every recess we would get into some dispute over a call. It typically went something like this:

"He was safe."

"No, he was out."

"Tie goes to the runner."

"But I got him just before he put his foot on the base."

This would continue for a couple of minutes until everyone's tempers were sufficiently flaring. A scuffle often occurred—like I said, we were hard-core. The recess monitors would gradually move to the scene, and then someone, most likely frustrated by the loss of precious recess time, would shout out: "DO-OVER!"

With these words, the debate would stop cold. Everyone would nonchalantly go back to where they started, and we would do the play all over again. It worked every single time. And generally all was forgotten (unless you were on the losing team and had to hear the "We're number one" cheer all the way back to class).

We have already mentioned that human beings need a Savior. They need someone who can pay the infinite debt that they incurred for sin, but can't "afford" to pay. They need someone who can put the pieces of their broken nature back together again. They need someone who can restore God's original plan for human beings found in *The Cosmic Prequel* so they can be fully human and find true happiness. They need the New Adam (Jesus) and the New Eve (Mary/the Church) to begin the new humanity (the baptized) that will live by the new rules (the Great Commandment/the Beatitudes), which are really the "original rules."

However, in order for humanity to go back to "the beginning," the New Adam and the New Eve must go back first. Jesus and Mary must *redo* everything that the first Adam and Eve did, but do it the right way, so they can *undo* everything that the first Adam and Eve did. The technical name for this is the redemption, but you could call it the divine do-over.

The bird's-eye view of the divine do-over goes something like this: Adam's "no" to God, which "led to condemnation for all people," was made possible through Eve's "no" to God. Likewise, Jesus' "yes" to God, which "leads to acquittal and life for all people," is made possible by Mary's "yes" to God (often called her "fiat"). But if we take a moment to "zoom in," we'll find some pretty amazing things.

Adam and Eve chose their will (what they decided was good and evil) over the Father's will in the Garden of Eden, refusing to love as God loves in and through their bodies. Due to this, Adam and Eve were destined to die and suffer the separation of their bodies and souls for all eternity. In addition, the consummation of the marriage of Adam and Eve, in which they became "one body," transmits to their offspring (all humanity) death and a damaged

Did U Know

Jesus taught that Baptism is necessary for salvation (Jn 3:5; CCC, no. 1257). However, in addition to the "baptism of water," the Church has understood that there is also the "baptism of blood," the "baptism of explicit desire," and the "baptism of implicit desire" (see CCC, nos. 1258–1260). These baptisms can "substitute" for the baptism of water where it is not possible for one reason or another.

nature that, without grace, is practically incapable of loving as God loves in and through the body.

Jesus and Mary, on the other hand, chose the Father's will (what God decided is good and evil) over their will in the Garden of Gethsemane (Jesus) and the garden in Nazareth (Mary). They both loved as God loves in and through their bodies: Jesus by offering his body on the cross and Mary by offering her body (and womb) as the mother of Jesus. Due to this, they were destined to live and enjoy the reunification of their bodies and souls for all eternity: Jesus in his resurrection and Mary in her assumption. And the con-summation of the marriage of Jesus and the Church (made on the cross and renewed in the Eucharist), in which they become "one body," transmits to their offspring (the baptized) life and a redeemed nature that is capable, by grace, of loving as God loves in and through the body.

> **For Your Consideration**
>
> Joseph was unwilling to "expose Mary to shame," which meant at best public humiliation and alienation, and at worst death by stoning. Interestingly, by telling Joseph, Mary reveals that she is "exposed" and "not ashamed." Could this also be a return to the original innocence before sin?

When we discover these "details" of the divine do-over, we can see clearly how our redemption—which includes the redemption of our bodies—is accomplished. First, you may notice that Mary, the New Adam's mother, is compared with Eve, the first Adam's wife. It's not important that Jesus and Mary were not husband and wife, as Adam and Eve were. What's important is that they are the "new man" and the "new woman." Jesus and Mary are the "model" man and woman, and everything that man and woman were supposed to be from "the beginning." *That's why they can give humanity a "new beginning."*

Did U Know
Mary is sometimes referred to as "co-redemptrix" or "cooperator in the redemption," and one of the Church's titles is the "Sacrament of Salvation." This doesn't mean that Mary redeemed us or that the Church saves us—obviously, Jesus does this. However, Jesus redeems us through Mary's "fiat" and saves us through the Church.

In addition, Mary, as the one who "housed" Christ in the "tabernacle" of her womb and bore him for the world, was a "model" of the Church. In fact, many of the same titles we give to Mary are also given to the Church, and vice versa. Maybe you've heard someone say "Holy Mother Church" before. Therefore, the Church can also be understood as the "New Eve." *The Church is the Bride of the New Adam* (Jn 3:27–29; Eph 5:21–33), and, as such, she becomes *the Mother of the faithful* who are reborn as sons and daughters of God from her "womb" in the waters of Baptism (Gal 4:4–7; Titus 3:4–7).

And that's where we come in.

The Sacrament of Baptism

The day of our baptism was the day "the greatest story ever told" became *our* story. It was the day when the divine do-over became *our* do-over.

I know that most of us were baptized as babies and probably don't remember it, but that was the most significant day in our lives. It was even more significant than the day we were born (although, obviously, that was a prerequisite). On the day of our Baptism, *everything changed* for us. We received a *new identity* and, with it, a *new power* and a *new hope* for the future. We also received a *new standard:* God's original plan from "the beginning." In Baptism, Jesus literally brought us "back to the beginning" and gave us a "new beginning."

So, how did Baptism accomplish all of this? At the very moment the water was poured over our heads, the Holy Spirit came into our hearts and we became identified with Jesus Christ and all that he accomplished in the divine do-over. We were joined to his saving death and resurrection in such a real and profound way that *we actually died and rose with him.* It's almost as if we were transported back in time and, in an instant, lived through it along with Jesus. This enabled *us* to receive *his merits* and reap the benefits of *his accomplishments* in the divine do-over. Pretty "mind-blowing," huh? That's because it's a *mystery,* and, as such, always lies beyond our total understanding. But one thing is for sure: it is very, very good news!

Becoming "Another Christ"

For all intents and purposes, this means that we have become *identified* with Jesus Christ; that *his* identity has become *our* identity. Therefore, each of us who has been baptized is, in a sense, *another*

Notable Quotable

"You see how many are the benefits of baptism...we have enumerated ten honors [it bestows]! For this reason we baptize even infants, though they are not defiled by [personal] sins, so that there may be given to them holiness, righteousness, adoption, inheritance, brotherhood with Christ, and that they may be his [Christ's] members."
— St. John Chrysostom

Christ. The original sin that marred our ability to live as God's image in the world and kept us from earthly and eternal happiness was forgiven, and we became the new man or the new woman, the visible "image of the invisible God" (Col 1:15) who has "hope of eternal life" (Titus 3:7). We became the son or daughter of God, conceived from the union of the New Adam and New Eve (Christ and the Church) and "born of water and the Spirit" (Jn 3:5) from her womb. As a result, we became members of the *People of God* and the *Family of God*, that is, the Church.

In a nutshell, through our "new beginning" in Baptism, we became everything we were created to be from "the beginning" *and more!* As a result, we are called and commanded to "live as Jesus lived" (1 Jn 2:6), love as Jesus loves (Jn. 15:12), and be holy as he is holy (see 1 Pet 1:14–16). Jesus himself set the *new standard,* and he is the yardstick by which we are to measure ourselves.

You may be thinking, "Then I'll never 'measure up.' That's an impossible standard." On one level you're absolutely right. We live as if in a tension between the first Adam and the last Adam. We are still left to battle the negative effects of sin on our nature and the influence of a world where "sin is in." The devil still "prowls around like a roaring lion" waiting to devour us (1 Pet 5:8). Each day we must fight temptation. Each day we must struggle against the tendency to lust instead of love and be selfish instead of selfless. Each day we must work to "put away the old self" (Eph 4:22 NAB) and "not be conformed to this world" (Rom 12:2). We become the new man or new woman in Baptism, but we also must become the new man or the new woman by the choices we make every day. That requires major effort on our part. "Working out our salvation" is a difficult task (see Phil 2:12). It demands a lifelong process and a long, hard road. And let's face it, if left to our own power and abilities (or rather, our own powerlessness and inabilities due to original sin), we would fail miserably. But there's more good news. Along with our *new identity* and our *new standard*, we received a *new power:* Jesus' power! We can do all things through Christ who strengthens us (see Phil 4:13). For human beings it is impossible to be the new man or new woman and live accordingly. But "with God all things are possible" (Mt 19:26; Mk 10:27; Lk 1:37). We are not in it alone.

Help from Heaven

In order to understand this better, let's use an analogy that Jesus used: a yoke. A yoke is a harness-like contraption that is fixed around the necks of oxen and attached to a plow for the oxen to pull. A yoke typically accommodates two oxen, so if one ox tires and can't pull the plow, the other ox will "pick up the slack" and finish the job. When Jesus says, "Take my yoke upon you...for my yoke is easy and my burden is light" (Mt 11:29–30), he is saying that being redeemed by him is like being "yoked" to him. He is in one side and we are in the other. And when, due to the effects of original sin, we find it difficult (or maybe even practically "impossible") to "love as God loves," Jesus "picks up the slack," provides what we lack, and *gives us grace* so that sin will not have dominion over us and we can "finish the job."

How does Jesus do this? He gives us a "helper" to *reorder* our inside-out and upside-down nature, to *recreate* us in his image, and to make up for what we lack (see Jn 14:16–17, 26). He gives us a "helper" who will ultimately *empower us to be the "helpers" God intended us to be for one another from "the beginning" as husband and wife!* This "helper" is the Holy Spirit, and we received him into our hearts on the day we were baptized! That's right: the same Holy Spirit who moved over the waters and created the world; the same Holy Spirit who was breathed into Adam and made him a living being; the same Holy Spirit who raised Jesus from the dead—dwells in us! Now that's real "power for living." Actually, it's real *power for loving.*

Remember how we said that the Holy Spirit is the "love of the Father and the Son" in the heart of the Trinity? That means that when we receive the Holy Spirit in Baptism, the "love of God" or *God's own love* comes to dwell in our hearts (see Rom 5:5). This divine love *gives us the power to "love as God loves"*: to give ourselves freely, totally, faithfully, and fruitfully in and through our bodies for the good of one another. He *enlightens our intellects* so we can once again know the truth about what is good. He *strengthens our wills* so we can choose it. He *quells the disordered passions of the body* so that the body will obey the commands of the soul. He transforms our bodies into "temples" through which we can offer ourselves in love as a "living sacrifice," just as Jesus did: "This is my body given for you." Yes, *we really can "love as Jesus (God) loves,"* because the "love with which the Father loves the Son and the Son loves the Father" is our "helper"! And if we can love as God loves, then we can fulfill the purpose of our existence as human beings and finally find the happiness we've been searching for.

And what can be better than that?

JOHN PAUL II
In His Own Words

Christ spoke in the perspective of the redemption of man and of the world (and, therefore, precisely of the redemption of the body). This is the perspective of the whole Gospel, of the whole teaching, of the whole mission of Christ.... Christ shares with believers his divine Sonship through the sacrament of Baptism.... The sacrament enables human beings to live the same life of the risen Christ.... Along with Christ's life Baptism fills the soul with his holiness.

(*GA*, 12/3/80 and 3/25/92, from
The Church: Mystery, Sacrament, Community,
[Boston, MA: Pauline Books & Media, 1998])

Things to Ponder and Share

1. Has there ever been a time in your life when you wished you could have a "do-over"? When and why?

2. Explain how Jesus is the New Adam and Mary/the Church is the New Eve.

3. What makes the redemption of human beings and the redemption of their bodies "good news"?

4. Try to find pictures of your Baptism day.
   Ask your parents about it. Who attended?
   What church was it held in? What were some
   of the gifts you received? Why did they choose
   your godparents? Ask your parents if they
   still have your baptismal gown, your "white
   garment," and your baptismal candle.

5. If possible, interview your godparents. Ask
   them how they felt when they were asked to
   take on that responsibility. How do they understand their special role in your life? How do
   they help you grow as a son or daughter of
   God and disciple of Jesus Christ?

6. If we in effect become "another Christ" in
   Baptism, then we should live as Jesus lived.
   Search the Gospels to find aspects of Jesus' life
   and character that you want to imitate. Then
   create a "mission statement" (a paragraph
   describing the sort of person you want to be)
   for your life based on Jesus' life. Keep it where
   you can read it every day as a reminder.

Read the
Catechism of the Catholic Church

nos. 504–507, 519–521, 615–618,
1262–1274, 1691, 1693–1696, 1701,
1708–1709, 1996–2000

CHAPTER 13

Tools of the Trade

Now the eleven disciples went to Galilee, to the mountain to which Jesus had directed them. And when they saw him they worshiped him; but some doubted. And Jesus came and said to them, "All authority in heaven and on earth has been given to me. Go therefore and make disciples of all nations, baptizing them in the name of the Father and of the Son and of the Holy Spirit, teaching them to observe all that I have commanded you; and lo, I am with you always, to the close of the age."

— Matthew 28:16–20

Help from the Church in Our New Life

I am about as mechanically dysfunctional as they come. Put me on stage in front of a crowd, and I am comfortable speaking to them. Sit me down at a computer to write, and it flows pretty naturally. But put a saw or a hammer in my hand, and I break out in a cold sweat. I've given up on doing home projects simply because they take me three times longer than people who actually know what they are doing. (And I usually have to call a professional anyway to fix the mess I've made.) Let's just say my kids don't buy me power tools for Father's Day.

My wife is the one in our house who knows how to swing a hammer, and she's always protesting that we don't have all the right tools in our toolshed. On more than one occasion she's lamented, "If I only had a table saw...." And you know—she's right! The right tools combined with the right "know-how" make all the difference in the world. Not only do they enable you to do the job correctly in the first place, but also in a fraction of the time it would have otherwise taken.

The same is true in the "new life" we began at our Baptism. When we were baptized, in a certain sense we "traded in" our *old self* for a *new and improved self.* As I mentioned in the last chapter, this new and improved self is fully equipped with the grace of the Holy Spirit. That grace enlightens our intellects to know what is good and strengthens our wills to choose it, so we can love as God loves. However, it should be fairly obvious that this knowledge and strength doesn't all come on the spot. On your baptismal day, you probably couldn't even talk or walk yet. Just as we do in our "natural" or physical life, in our *"supernatural"* or *spiritual life* we have to learn things and develop skills. In other words, *we need to acquire the right "know-how" and the right tools in our "new life."* Without them, we could

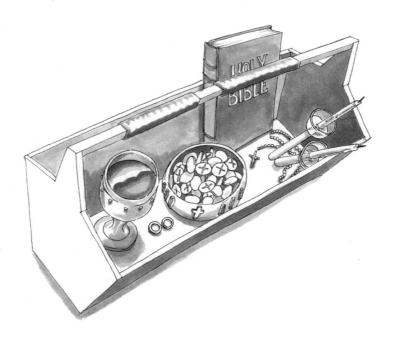

never do the job of loving as God loves and being holy as he is holy. With them, however, we cannot only do the job, but we can make great strides on the path of holiness. With them, we can overcome sin and temptation. With them, we can become the image and likeness of God we were intended to be from "the beginning."

So where do we get the right "know-how" and the "right tools"? We get them from our mother and teacher: the Catholic Church.

Sons and Daughters of the Church

You may have never thought of the Church as your mother before, but, believe it or not, that is indeed what the Church is. The Church is the Bride of Christ, the New Adam, who gave himself to her freely, totally, faithfully, and fruitfully in and through his body on the cross. She is the New Eve who is "fruitful and multiplies." She is the new "Mother of the living" who gives "birth" to sons and daughters of God in the waters of Baptism. *We* are those sons and daughters—

Notable Quotable

"Mother and Teacher of all nations—such is the Catholic Church in the mind of her Founder, Jesus Christ; to hold the world in an embrace of love, that men, in every age, should find in her their own completeness in a higher order of living, and their ultimate salvation."

— Pope John XXIII

and that makes the Church *our* mother! We are as much her sons and daughters as we are God's, for she is the one *through whom* we received "new life." Through our earthly mothers we received natural life; but through our spiritual mother, the Church, we receive divine life!

Without a doubt, mothers are our first and most important teachers. I don't mean to downplay the role dads have—after all, I am one—and studies have consistently shown the vital and necessary role that fathers play in the overall development of their children. But there's something special about moms. They not only "give us life," but they "teach us life." Mothers give us the right "know-how" in order to live. And because of this, we instinctively know that we should listen to them and that we owe them a special loyalty. Actually, we owe them *obedience.*

The word "obedience" comes from the Latin roots *ob* and *audio,* literally meaning "toward hearing." This reveals that obedience involves more than merely hearing words. It involves inclining your will *toward* what is heard and *choosing* it. So obedience means "listening *and* living."

The Church as our mother is our foremost teacher in the spiritual life. She "gave us new life" and she "teaches us new life." For this, we owe her a special loyalty. We should not only "hear her words," but we should "incline our wills toward them." In other words, we should obey her. After all, she is the one who gives us the right "know-how" so we can love as God loves in and through our bodies. And loving as God loves in and through our bodies will ultimately make us happy—both here on earth and forever in heaven. It's the key to a rich life! That's exactly what the Church wants for us and for "all nations." That's exactly what Jesus wants.

For this reason Christ gave the Church a share in his very own authority and power. He identified himself with her in such a profound way that when *she* speaks, *he* speaks. When we hear the Church speaking, *we are really hearing the voice of Christ* in her words. By his Spirit, Jesus is with his Church until the end of time and guides her to all truth (see Jn 16:13), making her "the pillar and bulwark of the truth" (1 Tim 3:15). This empowers the Church to "teach obedience to Christ's commands," or *teach life*, in addition to "making disciples of all nations" through Baptism, or *giving life*.

The Pope and Bishops:
True Teachers

The Church exercises this teaching authority through her "teaching office"—in Latin, *magisterium*. Christ established the magisterium when he declared to Peter that he was "the rock," gave him "the keys of the kingdom of heaven," and told him, "Whatever you bind [prohibit] on earth shall be bound in heaven, and whatever you loose [permit] on earth shall be loosed in heaven" (see Mt 16:18–19). Christ also gave this authority to "bind and loose" to all the apostles collectively (as a "college"—see Mt 18:18) and told them that "he who hears you hears me" (Lk 10:16). Peter individually and the apostles (including Peter) collectively speak on *behalf of* and with the *authority of* Jesus Christ. This isn't because Peter and the apostles were smarter than everybody else. It was because Jesus, by his Spirit, empowered them to do so, in order that all the faithful and all the world would know the truth that would set them free (Jn 8:32).

So who makes up the magisterium today? The *successors* of Peter and the apostles, that is, *the ones who hold their office:* the pope and the bishops. The pope individually and the pope and bishops collectively teach with the authority of Jesus Christ, and are therefore infallible in matters of faith and morals. That means that Jesus, by a special gift of the Holy Spirit, *guarantees* the truth of what they teach. This is why "the task of authentically interpreting the Word of God, whether written [Scripture] or handed on [tradition],"[7] belongs exclusively to them.

By now it should be clear how "Holy Mother Church," through her magisterium, teaches our intellects about what is good and provides us with the right "know-how." But as any caring mother does, the Church also assists us so we can put that "know-how" into practice. She does this by recommending the "right tools": prayer and the sacraments.

The First Tool for Our New Life: Prayer

Prayer can be defined as "the raising of one's mind and heart to God or the requesting of good things from God."[8] It can also be understood as communication with God who is our friend.[9] As such, communion with God is its goal. In relationships, the goal of communication is always communion. The more you communicate with someone, the closer

the two of you become. Just think of your closest
friend and the hours you spend either on the phone
or IMing one another!

This closeness often leads to "likeness."
Aristotle said that a close friend is "another self."
Have you ever noticed how close friends tend to
walk the same, talk the same, like the same things,
and finish one another's sentences? That's the consequence of spending a lot of "quality time" communicating with each other! It's almost as if they are
formed into each other's image. What do you think
would happen if you spent some serious quality
time communicating with God in prayer?

One aspect of prayer is requesting "good
things" from God, so what are the "good things"
that we should request from him? First, it is normal
and good to ask God for the necessities of our physical life, such as food, clothing, and shelter. It's also
good to ask God's help with our everyday activities,
whether at school, at work, at home, or on the ball-
field. Jesus told us to pray for such things, and he
wants us to pray for them. But Jesus also told us to
seek first the kingdom of God and his righteousness
(see Mt 6:33). The most important things to pray for
are those things that will help us to love as God
loves, as we hope to be with him in heaven one day.
We need to ask God to help us overcome temptation
and sin in our lives. We need to ask God to help us
keep his commandments and love our neighbor as
ourselves. We need to ask God to help us be "pure

in heart," as well as in body. God's word assures us that we will receive every grace we need: "Ask, and it will be given you..." (Mt 7:7). But we need to ask. We need to pray.

How Should We Pray?

Now that we've looked at what we should pray for, you may be wondering, "How should we pray?" Well, that's a great question. In fact, it's the very same question that Jesus' disciples asked him. In response, Jesus gave them (and us) the Our Father. This is *the fundamental Christian prayer* and should become the foundation for all our personal prayer. Think about it—Jesus is the one who gave it to us and told us, "When you pray, say Our Father...." That's why we call it the Lord's Prayer.

Actually, we will find that a number of the petitions of the Our Father are particularly pertinent to living God's plan for love, marriage, and sex, if we pray it thoughtfully and reverently .

In addition to the praying of the Our Father, we should invite the Blessed Mother into our prayer life. Why? Because Mary loved as God loves, in and through her body, more perfectly than any other human person, and she desires to help us do the same! Beyond that, as a model of the Church, she too is our Mother who loves us and who wants to obtain from her divine Son every grace we will need in order to fulfill the purpose of our existence and be happy in this life and in the life to come. Mary always presents our needs to Jesus, and Jesus, like a faithful son, always honors his mother's requests! So if we ask her to help us, we can be certain that she will rush to her Son with our request and that our request will be granted.

We could begin by praying the Hail Mary. Then, we can move on to one of the most powerful prayers, highly recommended by the Church and especially by Pope John Paul II (in fact, it was his favorite prayer): the Rosary. The vast number of saints and blesseds who have recommended the Rosary as a sure means to holiness is testimony to its importance for those desiring to live out God's plan for life, love, marriage, and sex.

The Second Tool for Our New Life: The Sacraments

In addition to prayer, we also need to receive the sacraments. The sacraments are channels of God's grace to us. They are vehicles of the Holy Spirit. They enable us to share in God's own life and love so we can be his image in the world. They are powers that come forth from the heart of our mother, the Church, that strengthen our wills to choose what is good. Simply put, *the sacraments empower us to love as God loves and live as Jesus lived.*

In their classic definition, the "sacraments are efficacious signs of grace, instituted by Christ and entrusted to the Church, by which divine life is dispensed to us" (CCC, no. 1131). That's a mouthful! But it sounds more complicated than it really is. The key is understanding what a *sign* is.

A *sign* is something that "points to" a particular reality that is present. For example, a "danger" sign means you're *actually in* danger. Therefore, the sacraments as *signs* "point to" a particular reality that is present in each of them. But, there's also something unique about the sacraments as signs: they *actually make* particular realities from the past—particular moments in salvation history—present to us here and now. It's almost like we are somehow transported back to these moments (or these moments are somehow transported forward to us) and we get the chance to really "live through them" personally. In the last chapter, we looked at how this is the case with the sacrament of Baptism.

Another quality about signs is that they are perceptible by the senses. This point is important. Human beings need the sacraments because we are *body-persons.* God meets us and comes to us through our bodies, through things we can see, hear, smell, taste, or touch—

For Your Consideration

The **Incarnation**—the Son of God becoming a man—is the most radical example of how God "meets" us in our humanity.

like water, oil, and bread and wine. The sacraments, therefore, are a testimony to how much God desires to be close to us!

In addition, the sacraments always "do what they signify." That is, the sign is "efficacious" or produces certain results or "effects" in us. This is because Jesus works in and through them. By the water Jesus cleanses us from sin; by the oil he strengthens the gifts of the Spirit in our souls; and by the bread and wine he nourishes our souls and makes us "one body" with him.

Jesus established these signs during his life as special and powerful ways for us to share in his life and love, and so that he could be with us always, "until the end of time." By sharing in the life of the Son of God, we can live as sons and daughters of God. By sharing in the life of the new man, we can live as new men and women. By sharing in the love of *the* "image of God," we can love as God loves and be the images of God we were created to be. By sharing in the love of the "Bridegroom of the Church," we can love freely, totally, faithfully, and fruitfully in and through our bodies, be true "helpers" to one another, and live out God's *original plan* for life, love, marriage, and sex!

Reconciliation and the Eucharist: As Often as We Need

In particular, we should make use of the grace available to us in the sacraments of Reconciliation and the Eucharist. Part of the beauty of these sacraments is that we can come to them as often as we need. And if we are serious about living out God's plan for us, we will need them often.

Frequently receiving the sacrament of Reconciliation is incredibly valuable. Not only do we receive the forgiveness of our sins, we also receive the grace we will need to avoid those sins in the future. That's right—confession not only gets rid of our sins, it fills us with grace! So we should try to go fairly regularly: once a month would be a good start. Of course, if we are aware of having committed a serious offense against God's commandments, we should go as soon as possible. My point is that we should be going on a regular basis as well, confessing even the little sins we commit every day. To give you an example, Mother Teresa and Pope John Paul II used to go to confession once a week. This was because their desire for holiness and purity was so great that they noticed even the smallest ways (probably undetectable to us) in which they failed to love as God loves, and they wanted God to help them to love more perfectly. We should follow their lead.

Then there's the great gift of the Eucharist. What could be more important in living God's plan for life, love, marriage, and sex than to receive the body and blood, soul and divinity of the spotless Lamb of God? Jesus desires to give himself to us, and with

> **For Your Consideration**
>
> Many parishes have set times for the sacrament of Reconciliation on Saturday afternoons, but you can also call your parish rectory and make an individual appointment.

him, every virtue he possesses! That means that when we receive Jesus in the Eucharist, we receive his love into our souls. If our desire is to love as Jesus loves, then receiving the Eucharist as often as we can is the surest and quickest way to do it.

If we can't get to Mass other than on Sundays, we can do two other things to receive the graces that flow from our Lord in the Eucharist. First, we can find a nearby church or chapel and visit him, for he is always waiting for us in the tabernacle. We can just spend some time sitting in his presence and ask him to help us be like him. Yet, if that isn't even possible, we can make an act of "spiritual communion," whereby we ask Jesus if he would become one with us spiritually since we can't receive his body and blood in Holy Communion. Jesus will honor the desire of our hearts and rush to be one with us so we can receive all the graces that Communion brings.

Working as if Everything Depends on Us

It's important to remember that having the right "know-how" and the right "tools" doesn't mean we don't have to put forth some major effort to live according to God's plan. Working out our salvation is a difficult task. In fact, St. Ignatius of Loyola said we must "work as if everything depends on us" and "pray as if everything depends on God." The real question is, "How bad do we want it?" Do we want the true happiness that only loving as God loves in and through our bodies can bring? If so, then we have to create a lifestyle that helps us do just that.

Maybe we will have to change some of the people we surround ourselves with and start walking with those who also want to live according to God's plan. Maybe we will have to find different social activities. Maybe we will have to change some of the movies or TV shows we watch, the books and magazines we read, the music we listen to, or the websites we surf. Maybe we will have to radically transform our approach to dating relationships.

But if we are willing to do our part, the "tools" are there to help us get the job done. Tools provided by a dear mother for her children: our mother, the Catholic Church, who loves us and wants us to be happy, both now and forever.

JOHN PAUL II
In His Own Words

By giving witness to the life of Christ, the "perfect man," the Church shows every person the way to realize his or her own humanity. Through her preaching she offers everyone an authentic model of life, and with the sacraments she instills in believers the vital energy which allows the new life to develop.

(*GA*, 5/20/92, from
The Church: Mystery, Sacrament, Community)

Things to Ponder and Share

1. Have you ever needed to accomplish a task and didn't have the right "know-how" or tools? Explain the situation and how this hindered your ability to do the job.

2. Outline how the Church is like a loving mother. Have you ever thought of this before? How do you think we should treat her as a result?

3. Explain the root words to "obedience." What does it mean when we claim that we are obedient to Mother Church?

4. How does the Church provide us with the right "know-how" so we can "love as God loves"? What is the magisterium? Who is part of it and why? Why is a "no" to the Church and her teachings (on matters of faith and morals) the same as a "no" to Christ and a "no" to real love? How have you regarded the Church's teachings in the past?

5. Define prayer in your own words. What are some of the definitions in the chapter? How do you pray? Why are the Our Father, the Hail Mary, and the Rosary powerful prayers? What do you think would happen if you spent some serious quality time communicating with God in prayer?

6. What is a sacrament? How are the sacraments like other signs? How are they different from

other signs? How can the sacraments—particularly Reconciliation and the Eucharist—help
you to be more like Jesus?

7. If we are to "work as if everything depends on
   us" while we "pray as if everything depends
   on God," what are some of the things in our
   lives that we may have to change in order to
   more effectively live out God's plan for life,
   love, marriage, and sex? Which of these do you
   find most challenging and why?

Read the
Catechism of the Catholic Church

nos. 880–896, 1123, 1127, 1129, 1131, 1391–1395,
1418, 1468, 2032–2036, 2673–2677, 2742–2745,
2761–2856

CHAPTER 14

A Model Marriage

> Be subordinate to one another out of reverence for Christ. Wives should be subordinate to their husbands as to the Lord...Husbands, love your wives, even as Christ loved the church and handed himself over for her.... This is a great mystery, but I speak in reference to Christ and the church.
>
> — Ephesians 5:21–22, 25, 32 NAB

A Sign of Christ's Love in the World

It is said that Henry Ford, the great automobile manufacturer and inventor of the famous Model T, was asked upon the occasion of his golden wedding anniversary, "To what do you attribute your fifty years of successful married life?" Ford replied, "The formula is the same one I've used in making cars: just stick to one model!"[10]

Although this may not be true of the Ford Motor Company any more, it is still true of marriage. There is indeed only one model: the marriage of Christ and the Church! This is the "great mystery" that each and every Christian marriage represents. This is the "example of love" that all Christian husbands and wives are commanded and empowered to follow. This is the "model marriage"—and we can "stick to it" because of the grace that flows from the sacrament of marriage.

It is commonly held that Jesus instituted the sacrament of marriage at the wedding at Cana in Galilee, where he performed his first miracle. Jesus' very presence at that wedding testifies to the goodness of marriage. And his celebrating the union of that Galilean couple with good food and good drink testifies to the joyfulness of the occasion (in fact, at a traditional Jewish wedding the celebration could last for days). However, these facts do not make marriage different than it had been before. They simply affirm what marriage already was: good and joyful. In order to raise marriage to new and glorious heights, something would have to change.

Enter the Blessed Mother. Mary approached Jesus with a potentially embarrassing situation for the newlyweds: the wine had run out. Jesus seems to answer her concern harshly, saying, "O woman, what have you to do with me? My hour has not yet come" (Jn 2:4). But Mary takes no offense. She just instructs the servants, "Do whatever he tells you" (Jn 2:5). Jesus then orders the servants to pour water into the stone jars that guests used for purification purposes (washing hands, feet, etc.). Let's just say as far as quality goes, this water couldn't compare with Poland Spring. Well, Jesus tells the servants to draw some out and bring it to the steward of the feast for him to taste. Could you imagine the terror that struck the servants at that very moment? They were probably thinking, "Bring the foot-washing water to the head steward to taste? Is this some kind of sick joke? We'll probably lose our jobs, not to mention get punished. We're going to be history— and all because of this Jesus from Nazareth!" They had no idea how right they were.

The response of the head steward must have shocked the servants: "This stuff is vintage! It is so generous of the newlyweds to save the best for last...and so unexpected, too." Imagine the servants standing there in amazement with gaping mouths as they thought, "You can say that again," and Jesus probably got a good laugh out of their reaction. I like to imagine that they started following the Lord that very day.

When Jesus changed the water into wine, he also changed "ordinary" marriage into something *extraordinary*. He made what had always been quite a *natural* thing for a man and woman to do—get married and raise a family—into a *supernatural* thing for a man and woman to do. It was at Cana in Galilee that Jesus identified the marriage of his followers with *his own marriage with the Church*—a marriage that would ultimately take place on the cross at Calvary.

Look carefully and notice the imagery in the story. Jesus calls Mary "woman," just like he does when he's on the cross: "Woman, behold, your son!" (Jn 19:26). Jesus refers to his "hour," which in John's Gospel always means the hour of his passion and death. And Jesus changes the water into wine, which prefigures the blood and water that flowed from his side and gave life to the Church.

The marriage of Christ and the Church on the cross is made present all over again when a baptized man and woman get married. The grace that flows from Christ's giving of himself—freely, totally, faithfully, and fruitfully in and through his body for the good of his Bride, the Church—enables Christian spouses to do the same through the sacrament of marriage. Because of this outpouring of grace, Jesus can command his followers to live out God's plan for marriage from "the beginning." They have become new men and women in Baptism, "remade" in the image of Jesus Christ, and therefore as spouses are to be *the physical image of the Trinity* and *the physical representation of Christ's love for the Church* in the world. And the sacrament of marriage makes all this possible.

Jesus Confirms and Renews
God's Original Plan for Marriage

Let's sum up the Creator's original plan for marriage, and show how Jesus, in his marriage to the Church, confirms it and renews it as the model that *all Christian marriages* must follow.

Marriage is...

- The *free* and *total* giving of a *man* and a *woman* to one another for each other's good, whereby they "belong" *exclusively* to one another.
- A pledge of *mutual help* and *support*.
- *Initiated* by means of *the spoken vows*, or *mutual consent*, blessed and approved by God.
- *Accomplished* (consummated) by means of *the body* through sexual union, which is the physical manifestation of the vows and the means through which the Holy Spirit *permanently binds* the spouses together, making them "one flesh."
- A *covenant* (as opposed to a mere contract), since by it *persons are exchanged* (as opposed to merely "goods and services"). Covenants are made between persons and God, whereas contracts are made solely between persons.
- A *communion of persons*.

- Directed toward the *procreation and education of children,* and therefore must always remain *open to the transmission of life.*

Jesus gives himself freely for his Bride, the Church. Speaking of his life, he said, "No one takes it from me, but I lay it down of my own accord" (Jn 10:18). He also gives himself totally for her good: he

Notable Quotable

"...The Church living with Christ who lives forever may never be divorced from him."
—St. Augustine

"emptied himself, taking the form of a servant" (Phil 2:7). Jesus shed his blood as a sign of the "new and everlasting covenant," accomplishing in his body what he had initiated in the vows he had made to Israel, namely, that he would be hers and she would be his (see Ex 6:7–8). When Jesus gives his body to his Bride, he becomes "one body" with her, and is permanently bound to her by the Holy Spirit (Jn 19:30). This communion with the Church gives life to "children of God" and educates them in the way of his commandments (Mt 28:19–20). And as much as Jesus' love is universal, it is also exclusive. St. Augustine once said that Jesus loves "each of us as if there were only us" and would have climbed on the cross if each of us were the *only* one to save.

So when a baptized man and woman get married, they are declaring that they accept God's original plan for marriage, confirmed and renewed by

Jesus Christ, and are committed to living according to this plan. This is the meaning of St. Paul's exhortation to Christian spouses to "be subordinate to one another out of reverence for Christ." And this is why at a wedding the couple actually declares their consent to what God has revealed to the Church *about* marriage before they give themselves to one another *in* marriage. They must testify that they know and understand, at least on a basic level, what they are getting into. The couple does this by answering these three questions that the Church asks them through her "official witness," the priest or deacon:

- Have you come here of your own free will and without reservation to give yourself to one another in marriage?
- Will you love and honor one another as husband and wife as long as you both shall live?
- Will you accept children lovingly as from God and raise them according to the law of Christ and his Church?

Do these questions sound familiar? For all intents and purposes, the priest or deacon could have asked, "Will you love each other freely, totally, faithfully, and fruitfully in and through your bodies, and thus be a physical image of the Trinity in the world and a sign of Christ's love for the Church?" And the answer must be a resounding, "Yes! We will."[11]

A "Yes" With Meaning

I say a *resounding* "yes" for a few very practical reasons. As already mentioned, by declaring their consent, the man and woman are saying that they understand what they are getting into when they enter marriage. Well, by their "yes," the man and woman are also saying that they are *free* and *able* to enter marriage (e.g., that they aren't already married, among other things). In fact, when the priest or deacon used to say, "If there is anyone present who knows why these two should not be joined in holy matrimony, let him speak now or forever hold his peace," he was really asking an honest question about the freedom of the man and woman to marry. The romanticized scene where another man bursts into the church out of breath at that very moment, saying, "Because I'm in love with her!" really has nothing to do with the question. If he said, "Because I'm married to her," *that* would be an issue.

A resounding "yes" is necessary as well because by it the man and woman are saying that they have *no reservations* regarding their marriage. This means that they are not withholding necessary and important information from each other that could seriously impact the other's choice of marriage. It also means that they are not placing any conditions on their promises: "I will love and honor you as my husband unless you do this," or "I will love and

honor you as my wife unless this happens." That's why the Church has always held that prenuptial agreements contradict what marriage is and that the couple who enters into one cannot enter into marriage. Marriage is permanent and unconditional.

If for any reason the couple is not able to answer a resounding "yes," then their marriage will not be *valid*. If their marriage is not valid, then they are not "lawfully" or truly married according to Christ and the Church. Experience shows that oftentimes the man and woman may not become fully aware that their "yes" wasn't genuine until years after the fact. This is why the Church recognizes annulments, but not divorce.

You may be wondering exactly what the difference is between an annulment and a divorce. It can be very confusing. Basically, if the man and the woman *are not* validly married, this can be recognized by the Church in what is called a "decree of nullity" or annulment. An annulment isn't a "Catholic divorce," nor is it something that the Church really "gives" to the couple. Rather, it is something that the Church declares to be the case: that the couple was never truly married in the first place. Hence, once they

> **Did U Know**
>
> It is true that a couple that receives an annulment still must get a civil divorce, but a civil divorce does not affect a validly contracted marriage. For a complete list of the requirements for a valid marriage, see Canon Law, nos. 1055–1165.

receive an annulment, both the man and woman would be free to marry someone else.

On the other hand, a divorce implies that there was indeed a marriage, but that it has been "broken," causing the man and woman to no longer be bound to one another. However, since God has revealed that in a valid marriage the Holy Spirit permanently binds the man and woman to one another (just as he binds the Father to the Son and Christ to the Church), the Church states that divorce is *impossible*. Therefore, if a man and woman *are* validly married, and then get divorced and marry someone else, they are technically committing adultery. This is the meaning of Jesus' words: "Whoever divorces his wife (unless the marriage is unlawful) causes her to commit adultery, and whoever marries a divorced woman commits adultery" (Mt 19:9 NAB).

Now, two questions often asked are: "Did the couple who got an annulment sin when they had sex, since they were not technically married?" and, "Are the children born to a couple who got an annulment considered 'illegitimate'?" Regarding the first question, there is no fault committed by the man and the woman because everyone, including the Church, presumed them to be validly married. The answer to the second question, therefore, is clearly "no." There aren't any "illegitimate" persons anyhow—God has willed us all and loves us more than we can possibly imagine!

Vows That Make a Marriage

Once the couple has declared that they accept and are committing themselves to what God has revealed to his Church about marriage and are entering into a valid marriage, they can go on to declare their consent to each other. It is here that the couple "confers" the sacrament of Marriage on each other. Contrary to popular belief, in the Roman Catholic Church the priest or deacon doesn't "marry" the couple. He *witnesses*, as an official representative of the Church, the man and the woman "marrying each other."

So, if the man and woman give the sacrament of Marriage to each other, what is the efficacious sign of the sacrament? The simple answer is *the marriage vows*. It is the vows *the spouses make* that *make them spouses*. However, these vows are actually expressed in two ways: through spoken language and through body language. You could say that in order for Marriage to take place, the man and woman must speak two languages.

If you have ever been to a wedding, I'm sure you have heard the spoken vows before: *I take you to be my lawful wife/husband, to have and to hold, from this day forward, for better, for worse, for richer, for poorer, in sickness and in health, until death do us part.* In a nutshell, these words are a solemn promise by the spouses to "freely give themselves for the good of one another," without any conditions or reservations, for "as long as they both shall live." That means that every day they will choose to sacrifice themselves for what is truly good for the other person—even if it doesn't "feel" good, and even if the other person doesn't return it or particularly deserve it. In a sense, spouses say to each other: "*Your good* is my command."

After the man and woman exchange spoken vows, they exchange rings. These rings are not *efficacious signs*, but they are signs nonetheless. They "point to a reality that is present": the marriage of the couple enacted by the vows they exchanged. Yet, it is important to note that it is by the vows that the man and woman are married, not by the rings. That's why in a Catholic marriage the man and woman do not say, "With this ring I thee wed," but, "Receive this ring, as a sign of my love and fidelity, in the name of the Father, and of the Son, and of the Holy Spirit."

At the very moment when the man and the woman give themselves to one another freely, totally, faithfully, and fruitfully in their vows, their relationship undergoes a transformation. It is now that they "belong" to each other. It is now that they are spouses. God then blesses and approves this "exchange of persons" and "mutual belonging" through his representative, the priest or deacon. That is why it is at this point and only at this point that God's representative pronounces the couple "man and wife."

He then says the much anticipated words: "You may kiss the bride." Now, you may be tempted to think that since the deal has been "sealed with a kiss," that that's the end. But while the marriage has been *initiated*, it hasn't been *accomplished*. The sacrament of Marriage has been *conferred*, but it hasn't been *completed*. To become "one flesh," the man and the woman will actually need to become one flesh.

That is, they are going to have to speak a second language.

JOHN PAUL II
In His Own Words

Through marriage as a sacrament [Christian spouses] participate in Christ's saving love.... In the light of Ephesians—precisely through participation in this saving love of Christ—marriage as a sacrament of the human "beginning" is confirmed and at the same time renewed.

(*GA*, 12/15/82)

Things to Ponder and Share

1. Before people build a house or a car, they usually make a model. What is the purpose of having a model?

2. Have you ever experienced God changing water into wine in your life: making what is ordinary into something extraordinary? Explain the situation.

3. How does the marriage of Christians represent the marriage of Christ and the Church? What are some ways that Christian spouses can love one another as Christ loves the Church?

4. Why is it so important for anyone seeking marriage to understand and accept God's plan for marriage from "the beginning"? Why is it so important that they are *able* to understand and *freely* accept it?

5. In the sacrament of Marriage, words transform the relationship. Have you ever experienced the power of words to transform a relationship in your life, for better or for worse? When and how?

6. Why is it significant that a man and a woman belong to each other only when they become spouses?

Read the ——————————
Catechism of the Catholic Church

nos. 1601, 1613, 1615–1617,
1625–1632, 1643–1651,
2382–2391

CHAPTER 15

Body Language

The body, however, is not for [sexual] immorality, but for the Lord, and the Lord is for the body.... Avoid [sexual] immorality. Every other sin a person commits is outside the body, but the [sexually] immoral person sins against his own body. Do you not know that your body is a temple of the holy Spirit within you, whom you have from God, and that you are not your own? For you have been purchased at a price. Therefore, glorify God in your body.

— 1 Corinthians 6:13b, 18–20 NAB

Sex That Tells "the Truth"

I'm sure that you have heard the phrase "actions speak louder than words." It's a clever and concise way of saying that our body language and our spoken language need to "say" the same thing. Our body language is often "louder" because it can either fulfill or contradict what our words have said. We can see this most vividly in the "language of the body" spoken by a man and a woman in sexual union.

Before we go on, however, we need to ask ourselves a question: What is the whole purpose of language in the first place? It's communication, of course. Communication is extremely important. Remember how from "the beginning" human beings were created in the image of the Trinity *as persons* for a *communion of persons?* It would be pretty difficult to form a communion of persons if we couldn't communicate with each other. So you could say that *language helps us to fulfill the purpose of our existence!* Actually, only a certain kind of language does: one that *communicates truth.*

It's only when two persons freely give themselves for *what is truly good* for each other that they "become one" with each other. A "communion of persons" based on lies and falsehoods wouldn't be a communion at all. This is why *truth-telling is an essential part of being human:* we can't love as God loves and form a communion of persons without it. And since we are body-persons, we must "tell *the truth*"—not *my* truth or *your* truth—with our words *and* with our bodies.

But what is *the truth* that the "language of the body" is supposed to "tell" in the sexual union of a man and a woman? It's supposed to say, "I am yours and you are mine!" Right from "the beginning," sexual union was meant to express mutual belonging and communicate a love that is free, total, faithful, and fruitful. In the last chapter we learned that a man and woman only "belong" to

each other *after* they exchange vows and those vows are blessed and approved by God through his representative, the priest or deacon. This is because when a couple exchanges their vows they are in fact exchanging their persons. They are giving themselves to one another—freely, totally, faithfully, and fruitfully—for each other's good. Since only spouses belong to each other, only they have rights to one another's bodies in a sexual way (see 1 Cor 7:3-4). This is actually the full meaning of the Sixth Commandment, "You shall not commit adultery," which is more properly understood as prohibiting sexual relations with anyone who is not your spouse—that is, with anyone who does not belong to you and to whom you do not belong. Therefore, the "language of the body" in sexual union can only "tell the truth" *if the man and woman are spouses.*

In addition, sex is supposed to be *the marriage vows communicated in body language.* The words of the spoken vows—"I give myself to you: freely, totally, faithfully, and fruitfully, in and through my body for your good. I desire to be one with you and form a life-giving communion of persons"—are fulfilled in the sexual union of the spouses. The "sign" of the sacrament of Marriage is complete only when the marriage vows have been expressed in both spoken language and body language. And since the sacraments always "do what they signify," when a baptized man and woman become "one body" in sexual union, *they actually become "one body."* It is through their first sexual union after their spoken vows have been blessed and approved by God and his Church that the Holy Spirit joins the man and woman in a permanent and unbreakable bond (often called an *indissoluble* bond). And this is precisely why sexual union completes and accomplishes (or *consummates*) the marriage.

You may also recall that signs point to a reality that is present (e.g., a "danger" sign means you are in danger), but that the sacraments as signs actually *make* certain realities present. If that's the case, what realities does the sign of the sexual union of Christian spouses point to and make present?

In God's original plan for marriage and sex, the sexual union of spouses was supposed to be the image of the life-giving communion of persons within the Trinity (remember Adam and Eve?). Due to sin, sexual union lost its capacity to signify the communion of persons within the Trinity. But through the death and resurrection of Jesus Christ and his gift of the Spirit of love received in Baptism, the communion of Christian spouses in sexual union once again signifies the communion of persons within the Trinity.

In Christ, the communion of spouses also receives a new significance: it represents the "holy communion" of Christ and his Bride the Church. This communion was supremely expressed when he gave himself freely, totally, faithfully, and fruitfully in and through his body on the cross. On the cross Jesus accomplished or *consummated* his marriage with the Church, and he memorializes and renews it in the Eucharist. Becoming "one body" with the Lord in Holy Communion strengthens our bond with Christ and imparts grace to us for living the Christian life. Similarly, each and every sexual "communion" between Christian spouses, after the one that consummates their marriage, memorializes and renews their marriage. Becoming "one body" in sexual communion strengthens the bond between the spouses and imparts grace to them for living the Christian married life. That's right...for Christian spouses, sex is a means of God's grace!

Only Marital Sex Tells "The Truth"

It should be clear that in order for the body language of sexual union to tell "the truth," it must be *between a man and a woman who are spouses* and it must be *a genuine expression of free, total, faithful, and fruitful love.*

Put another way, sex must be *marital.* You may have heard people say that *premarital* sex (fornication) or *extramarital* sex (adultery) are evil and against God's plan for marriage and sex. However, it is actually more precise to say that *nonmarital* sex is evil and against God's plan for marriage and

> **For Your Consideration**
>
> The virtue of chastity is best understood as a great "yes" to God's plan for life, love, marriage, and sex. The chaste person "tells the truth" with his or her body. That's why chastity is for everyone— whether the person is single, a priest or religious, or married.

sex.[12] This, of course, would include any sexual relations that are premarital or extramarital, but it would also include any sexual relations *between spouses* that are not a genuine expression of free, total, faithful, and fruitful love. Being spouses, of course, is necessary for the sexual union of a man and woman to be marital, but it is not sufficient. Their sexual union must also be an accurate portrayal of their marriage vows to love as God loves.

> **For Your Consideration**
>
> An in-depth treatment of all the differences between marital and nonmarital sex is beyond the scope of this book. However, a brief overview is important in order to see how these issues are framed in light of the Theology of the Body.

Those who engage in *marital* sex "tell the truth" with their bodies, while those who engage in *nonmarital* sex *do not*. And when I say sex must be marital, I mean *all sexual relations*, not just intercourse. With this in mind, let's look at the difference between marital and nonmarital sex.

Exclusively for Husband and Wife

Obviously, in order for sex to be "marital," the man and the woman *must actually be married*. With this in mind, we can see why it is wrong for those who are engaged to be married to "engage" in sexual relations. Since the engaged to be married *aren't married,* their sexual union can never be marital and therefore cannot "tell the truth." Engaged persons may have made a promise of marriage, but they haven't made *the promises of marriage,* that is, they haven't exchanged *marriage vows.* As a result, there's nothing for their sexual relations to express, memorialize, or renew. They aren't spouses; they do not "belong" to each other. Not yet, anyway.

Also, in God's plan for creation, *a man and woman* are the only ones who can become "one flesh" and form a *life-giving communion of persons* through sexual union. From "the beginning," sexual complementarity is not something *accidental* to marriage, but rather something *essential* to marriage (see chapter 6). Sexual union is only truly possible for a man and a woman. Two persons of the same sex may perform bodily sexual acts, but they cannot become "one body." That total self-giving requires *sexual complementarity.* As a result, it is impossible for two persons of the same sex to be spouses. They cannot become "one flesh" in marriage because they cannot become "one flesh" in sexual union and because their sexual acts, *by their very nature,* can never be life-giving and become a "third person."

This in no way implies that those who struggle with homosexual feelings or tendencies shouldn't be treated with love. Of course they should—they

Did U Know

Biologically, sexual intercourse (coitus) refers to the joining of the male and female sexual organs. It implies sexual difference. That's why it is technically impossible for homosexuals to have sexual intercourse. Therefore, it is more accurate to use the term "homosexual acts" instead of "homosexual sex."

are *persons*. Neither does it indicate that homosexual feelings or tendencies, though disordered, are in themselves sinful. People don't tend to choose such feelings and tendencies, and those who wrestle with them deserve our compassion and assistance. However, it does explain why homosexual *acts* and "gay marriage" contradict the very meaning and purpose of marriage as a sign of the Trinity and of Christ's union with the Church. Jesus himself affirmed that God's plan from "the beginning" was for marriage to be between one man and one woman when he said, "Have you not read that from the beginning the Creator *'made them male and female'*...and *'the two shall become one flesh'?"* (Mt 19:4–5 NAB) So those who engage in homosexual acts do not tell *the truth* with their bodies.

> **Check It Out**
>
> Ministries like COURAGE (http://couragerc.net) assist men and women with same-sex attractions in living chaste lives.

Marital sex is free. In order for sex to be marital it must be *freely chosen*. Sex cannot be forced upon someone. This is called rape—and it is a horrific violation of a person's dignity. It should go without saying that a person who has been violated in this way bears no moral fault. Sadly, so many rape victims blame themselves for something *they didn't do*, but rather that was *done to them*.

Sex being freely chosen also means that a person cannot be manipulated or tricked into engaging in sexual relations. This can happen when one person puts pressure on the other, or makes the person feel guilty, or lies to him or her, or offers sex as a reward or withholds it as a punishment. It can also happen when a person tries to get the other to drink alcohol or take drugs for the very purpose of limiting that person's inhibitions.

Sex also would not be freely chosen when it is simply the result of sexual instincts or drives. While there's no doubt that people are more "in the mood" at certain times than others, to have sex solely in response to the body's impulses really resembles the way animals behave, as opposed to the way humans behave as body-persons. To act in this way would amount to the man and the woman using one another to fulfill their sexual urges, which is anything but love.

Marital sex is total. In order for sex to be marital it must be *the total gift of oneself* to the other. The man and woman must give their bodies, their minds, and their hearts. There cannot be any reservations. Sex cannot be a "partial gift." This can happen, for example, when sex is the result of lust.

The *Catechism of the Catholic Church* defines lust as "disordered desire for or [excessive] enjoyment of sexual pleasure" (no. 2351). Now, it is important to note that mere sexual attraction is not the same thing as lust. There's nothing disordered about a man being sexually attracted to a woman and vice versa, especially when they are spouses. And sexual pleasure is good—it was God's idea, after all. Sexual pleasure becomes *disordered* when it is sought for its own sake. And that's exactly what lust does (see chapter 10).

If someone has lust for their spouse, they view him or her as an object for their own sexual gratification. This isn't a *giving* at all, but rather a *taking*. If someone has lust for a person who is not their spouse, they clearly wouldn't be giving their mind and heart totally to their spouse, which is what they promise in their marriage vows. That's why Jesus said, "Everyone who looks at a woman lustfully has already committed adultery with her in his heart" (Mt 5:28).

The total gift of oneself must also be expressed authentically in and through the body. This means that sexual stimulation and sexual climax can only "tell the truth" when they are *fulfilled in sexual union*. If treated as "ends in themselves," apart from the one flesh union of spouses and its life-giving capacity, they are simply not marital. This brings to light why masturbation has no place in God's plan for our sexuality. It also shows us that the sexual acts that prepare the spouses' bodies for intercourse and are intended to sexually stimulate them—commonly called foreplay—cannot be separated from sexual union. Spouses who engage in such acts apart from or in place of sexual union use one another exclusively for individual sexual pleasure and purposely choose not to become "one body." They intentionally make the gift of sex a "partial gift," in effect saying, "You can have 'all' of me, except my fertility."

No matter how one might try to justify it, this is just not an accurate portrayal of the marriage vows or a genuine expression of a total love.

Marital sex is faithful and exclusive. In order to be marital, sex must also express *faithfulness and exclusivity.* Sex must say, "It's you and only you!" Sex must also say, "I'm true to my word!" There's no such thing as "Christian swingers" or "open" relationships. This is *not* what I meant when I said that love is radically inclusive! There are no "third parties" in marital sex. That goes for our minds and hearts as well. It should also be obvious that adultery violates the faithful and exclusive nature of sex. It should also be obvious that viewing pornography, or deliberately viewing with knowledge of their content magazines, books, movies, television programs, websites, and music videos that aren't "technically" pornography but that nevertheless depict the human body in a lustful way and inspire "adultery in the heart," would also violate the faithful and exclusive nature of sex.

> **For Your Consideration**
>
> One of the largest growing problems today is pornography addiction, particularly online. Pornography constitutes some 12% of total websites, accounts for 25% of all online searches, and makes some 57 billion dollars worldwide annually.

Finally, *any* breaking of the free, total, or fruitful aspects of marital sex is a breaking of the marriage vows and so also a violation of faithfulness. In other words, you are saying with your body that you didn't really mean what you said in your words at the altar.

Marital sex is willingly fruitful. In order to be marital, sex must be *willingly fruitful.* That is, the spouses must always remain open to becoming parents and never do anything that *directly and intentionally causes* any sexual union to be infertile. This would include sexual acts that are brought to climax apart from sexual union. It would also include sexual acts that *by their very nature* are incompatible with procreation, such as those between two persons of the same sex. And it would include "any action which either before, at the moment of, or after sexual intercourse, is specifically intended to prevent procreation" (Pope Paul VI, *Of Human Life,* no. 14).

> **For Your Consideration**
>
> **Helps to Break Free from Porn Use:**
> 1. Destroy all pornography in your possession.
> 2. Obtain a server level Internet filter.
> 3. Find a friend to whom you can be accountable.
> 4. Seek spiritual direction.
> 5. Receive the sacraments of Reconciliation and Eucharist often.
> 6. Pray hard—especially to Mary and the saints.

Plainly put, contracepted sex—whether it utilizes a pill or a patch, a condom or a cup (diaphragm), a spermicide, a sponge, a shot, or simple withdrawal—is a violation of the fruitful nature of love and a contradiction of the marriage vows. Spouses who engage in such nonmarital sex do not "tell the truth" with their bodies. By directly and intentionally preventing their love from becoming a "third person" in the child and refusing to be "pro" God's creation, they are in effect saying to each other, "I do not really want to become 'one flesh' with you." Not only that, they actually might be killing their own flesh.

Contraception or Abortion?

Most chemical "contraceptives," like birth control pills, contraceptive patches, or injections, act as *abortifacients.* That means that they can cause a very early abortion, usually by making the implantation of the newly conceived human being impossible by disrupting the uterine lining. This is a "backup plan" built into these drugs, just in case they fail to work in their contraceptive capacity. When you consider the number of women who use chemical "contraceptives," and that at least some of the time they act as abortifacients, it's almost mind-boggling to think about how many babies really die every year by abortion—since there are about 1.3 million surgical abortions performed in the United States every year and over 30 million performed world-wide.

It's important to remember that the *fundamental task* of marriage is to serve life. Children are always a blessing and never a burden. They are not a disease to be eradicated by taking a pill. The conception of a child is when sexual union most fully manifests its splendor and when the "language of the body" speaks the loudest.

Marriage, by its very nature as an image of the Trinity, is supposed to be a family affair.

JOHN PAUL II
In His Own Words

Marriage is a sacrament which is contracted by means of the word..."I take you as my wife—as my husband...."[However, it] can be fulfilled only by means of conjugal [marital] intercourse.... Thus then, from the words whereby the man and the woman express their willingness to become "one flesh,"...we pass to the reality which corresponds to these words. Both the one and the other element are important in regard to the structure of the sacramental sign.... The structure of the sacramental sign remains essentially the same as in "the beginning." It is determined by the language of the body.... By means of the body, the human person is husband and wife.

(GA, 1/5/83 and 3/12/80)

Things to Ponder and Share

1. Describe a time in your life when your actions "spoke louder than your words."

2. Why is "truth-telling" such an important part of human language and human existence?

3. When those who aren't married engage in sexual relations, they *do not* "tell the truth"

with their bodies. Why? How does this relate to the Sixth Commandment, "You shall not commit adultery"?

4. In order for the *body language* of sexual union to "tell the truth," it must be marital. What makes sex marital?

5. Give examples of marital sex and nonmarital sex.

6. How does God's plan for sex differ from what is so often "communicated" in society and in the media? Can you think of an example where God's plan for sex was the same as what is communicated in society and in the media? Share specific examples.

Read the ———————————
Catechism of the Catholic Church

nos. 1640, 2332, 2336,
2350–2363

CHAPTER 16

A Family Affair

Blessed is every one who fears the LORD, who walks in his ways! You shall eat the fruit of the labor of your hands; you shall be happy, and it shall be well with you. Your wife will be like a fruitful vine within your house; your children will be like olive shoots around your table.... Lo, sons are a heritage from the LORD, the fruit of the womb a reward. Like arrows in the hand of a warrior are the sons of one's youth. Happy is the man who has his quiver full of them!

— Psalms 128:1–3, 127:3–5a

The Role of the Christian Family in the World

My favorite baseball team of all time is the 1979 Pittsburgh Pirates. Even though we lived in New Jersey, my dad was born and raised in Pittsburgh, and that meant that I really had no say in the matter—somehow genetically I was both a Pirates and a Steelers fan. Being the devoted son of a Steel-town native, I passionately rooted every game. I had my Steelers "terrible towel" in my hand in the winter and wore my "Bucs" square-top baseball cap on my head all summer.

Then came the year to rival all years: 1979. That year the Steelers had defeated the Dallas Cowboys in Super Bowl XIII by a three-point margin, and our beloved Pirates slugged their way to the World Series. They faced the Baltimore Orioles, and to tell you the truth, the first half of that series cast a pall over the Hajduk house. The Pirates were down 3–1, and no team in Major League history had ever come back from that kind of a deficit. As much as we might have doubted, however, we never lost hope. And it was all because of the Pirates' motto during that season: "We Are Family."

I can still see Willie Stargell (arguably one of the best homerun hitters ever and the veteran of the squad affectionately known as "Pops") pulling the team together. I can still hear that song by Sister Sledge: "We are family...." The fans got up and sang at good ol' Pops' bidding. Everybody was united. Everybody believed. Everybody supported and encouraged each other—fans and players alike. We followed Pops' lead—and it wound up making baseball history, as the Pirates rallied to win three straight! As silly as it sounds, I cried that day. I think my father did too.

Remember how I said that by its very nature as an image of the Trinity (the First Family) marriage is supposed to be a family affair? This is also true of its nature as an image of Jesus' marriage with the

Church—a union that created the ever growing "family of God" through the "birthing waters" of Baptism. Marriage and sex are not just about a "you" and a "me"—they're about a "we." For this reason, sexual union always includes and never intentionally excludes the "third person" of the child. In a sense, in each and every sexual union the man and woman recognize and rediscover the profound meaning of their masculinity and femininity. By joining together in such an intimate way as to become "one flesh," they open themselves up to the fullest realization of that "one flesh" union: the conception of a child. That is, they open themselves up to the *possibility* of fatherhood and motherhood. Fundamentally, they say with their bodies as well as their souls, "We are family. We will—if God wills— no longer to be two, but three." This is all part of what spouses communicate in the "body language" of sexual union.

The Mission of the Married

"Be fruitful and multiply" (Gen 1:28) was the original blessing of the Creator not only on the first married couple, but also on every married couple that would be modeled upon them. In God's plan, the heavenly Father calls spouses to cooperate with him in the task of enlarging and enriching *his own*

> **Check It Out**
>
> For more about God's plan for spouses to cooperate with him, read John Paul II, *The Role of the Christian Family in the Modern World*, no. 28.

family. Through their openness to life, spouses actually participate in the awesome mission of creating new persons made in God's image and likeness; the mission of creating "kids for the kingdom." Thus, the fundamental task of the family is to serve and foster life: both natural life and eternal life. This is why the procreation and education of children are not something "added onto" marriage, but are rather at the very heart of marriage itself!

Since the family has this fundamental task to serve and foster both natural and eternal life, it has the responsibility to proclaim and share the Gospel, to teach and learn love, and to provide for the needs of earthly life. The family, sometimes called the domestic Church, can, in a very real and true way, claim for itself the titles and the mission assigned to the Church. The family is a "sacrament of salvation" that "makes Christ present" in the world. As such, it is called to proclaim the Gospel in word and deed, teach obedience to God's commandments, witness to the sanctity of life, set an example of love, and serve the poor and vulnerable. The Christian family indeed has a mission and a ministry—first to its members, since "charity begins at home," but then to the Church and to the world!

Parents, by virtue of the fact that they are parents, have the inalienable right and irreplaceable duty to educate their children and form them in the faith. They are the first and most important teachers that their children will ever have. They are respon-

sible not only for the physical well-being of their children—food, clothing, shelter, education, health care and the like—but also for the spiritual well-being of their children. That means that Christian parents must, to the best of their ability, ensure that their children come to know, love, and serve the Lord Jesus and his Church. They need to work diligently to preserve and protect the baptismal purity of their children and help them to develop a firm resolve to avoid sin in their lives and seek holiness. Parents should be zealous for the eternal salvation of their kids. Their primary task is to form saints, not necessarily scholars; to help their children get to heaven, not necessarily Harvard. That's not to say that parents shouldn't be concerned with their children's educational future or that they should somehow be disappointed if their children go to a dynamite school. Neither does it mean they should undervalue the material needs of the body. But it does mean that parents need to put "first things first." Life is short. Eternity is...well...eternal. And all temporal goods find their true value only in light of their ultimate purpose: to equip us to love as God loves in and through our bodies; to empower us, through our unique and individual giftedness, to be an unrepeatable physical image of God in the world.

Therefore, this total formation as a human being, body and soul, is really meant to enable children to become *the gifts that they are:* gifts for the

Church *and* for the world. Parents are called to raise their children to become productive members of society who will offer their gifts, indeed *offer themselves,* to help transform what Pope John Paul II called the "culture of death" into a "culture of life and love," by promoting all that is good, true, and beautiful. In so doing, the family clearly shares in the life and mission of the Church and participates in the development of society, which are two more of its tasks (cf. John Paul II, *The Role of the Christian Family in the Modern World,* no. 17). The family is the school of love, where children learn to give themselves freely, totally, faithfully, and fruitfully in and through their bodies for the good of others. The family is the domestic Church in which parents nourish their children with the Word of God and teach them all that Jesus commanded, so they can become co-workers with the Holy Spirit in building up God's kingdom and in renewing the face of the earth!

> **Did U Know**
> Parents, called to give themselves freely, totally, faithfully, and fruitfully in and through their bodies for the good of their children, learn daily what it means to love as Jesus loves. Since loving as God loves is the way to be fully human and happy, this is how children contribute to the good of their parents. In fact, children help parents live a rich life and get to heaven!

Responsible Parenthood

Now, you may wonder: if the fundamental task of the family is to serve and foster life, are there ever

times when having another child might actually *not* serve and foster life? The short answer is "yes." That's why the Church speaks about "responsible parenthood." However, we need to properly understand exactly what that means.

"Responsible parenthood" means that spouses are called to intelligently and willfully cooperate with God in the procreation of children. They are not called to merely submit themselves to biological processes, but rather to act, in a certain sense, as "interpreters" of God's plan by carefully considering their genuine good and that of their family.

This is why the Church has never proposed that a couple should have as many children as physically possible. While children are always a blessing and never a burden, having more children than one can reasonably provide for would be plain *irresponsible* and would demonstrate a lack of consideration for the good of the family. There may be serious and just reasons why Christian spouses may decide to refrain from conceiving another child for the time being.

Notice that I said "serious and just" reasons and "for the time being." Unless a couple has serious and just reasons to avoid having children, they shouldn't do anything to avoid having them. Rather, they should welcome children with "the generosity appropriate to responsible parenthood." However, if a couple has "serious and just" reasons, they may find it necessary to avoid conceiving a child until these reasons no longer exist. Clearly, such reasons could exist for quite a long time, even indefinitely. But the couple should take the view that this time of avoiding the conception of a child is temporary and not permanent; that they are *postponing* children and not *excluding* them.

"Serious and Just" Reasons vs. the "Contraceptive Mentality"

It is important to note that these serious and just reasons have little to do with "lifestyle" or "social status." They have to do with *hardship*. If such reasons were about "lifestyle" or "social status," they wouldn't be "serious" or "just" at all, but would merely be a disguise for materialism or for what John Paul II called a "contraceptive mentality."

A contraceptive mentality does not approach the conception of children with openness and generosity. It tends to pit human life itself against a variety of personal goals: career, class, financial independence, material possessions, and the like. Those who think in this way select the number of children they will have (if they decide to have any at all) according to the lifestyle they wish to maintain. Sometimes, both parents go off to work (while their children get dropped off at day care) not because they cannot "make ends meet" any other way—which would be justifiable—but because they are unwilling to sacrifice their careers or their lifestyle. A contraceptive mentality suffers from inverted thinking and betrays, whether consciously or not, an *anti-life* attitude that treats persons as objects rather than gifts and views procreation as an obstacle to personal fulfillment. It is easy to see how abortion becomes an extension of the contraceptive mentality and the "only possible decisive response to failed contraception."[13] And it's fair to say that there may be nothing that contradicts God's original plan for human love, human sexuality, marriage, and family life more than abortion, for it involves the utter denial of God as the sovereign Lord of life and the refusal to freely, totally, and faithfully give oneself to another person in order to *give them life.*

A married couple also shouldn't postpone conceiving children out of a misguided, albeit understandable, desire to give their children everything—whether it be the best clothes, the best "toys," or providing full tuition for the best college. The truth is that the greatest "treasures" you can give your children are brothers and sisters! I've never met a person who came from a large family who didn't love it or who would have "traded" their brothers and sisters for more stuff or their own room.

All this being said, let me share some examples of what might be serious and just reasons to postpone pregnancy. Some cases involve emotional or physical sickness or hardship. In other situations, parents justly desire to space their children for the emotional and physical well-being of the mother. A family could be facing financial difficulties that make it practically impossible to reasonably provide for the basic needs (food, clothing, shelter, etc.) of the children they already have. Sometimes an already living child is very ill or has a disability that requires much time, attention, and resources. Some marriages become unstable, especially where there is spousal abuse, lack of spousal support, or domestic violence. These are just some examples of serious and just reasons.[14] Unfortunately, not all situations are equally easy to determine. That's why the Church teaches that, ultimately, the couple themselves must decide whether they have serious and just reasons to postpone pregnancy. They make this prudential judgment in prayer, mindful of the moral principles the Church proposes, and with a careful examination of their motives.[15] The Church recommends seeking the advice of friends and family, as well as that of a spiritual director (like a priest, religious

Did U Know

For just reasons, spouses may wish to space the births of their children. It is their duty to make certain that their desire is not motivated by selfishness but is in conformity with the generosity appropriate to responsible parenthood (cf. CCC, no. 2368).

sister, or a lay professional) before reaching a conclusion. At the same time, the Church also encourages families to trust in the Lord to provide for their
needs, even in the midst of hardship.

Natural Family Planning: Faithful to the Marriage Vows

What if a couple determines that they have serious
and just reasons to avoid conceiving a child for the
time being? If sexual union must always be *willingly fruitful* in order to be marital, does that mean that
that couple must abstain from sexual relations until
those serious reasons cease to exist? The answer is
yes and no.

Admittedly, this may not seem like much of an
answer. If we review the foundational principles of
marital union, we see that while each and every
marital act is an expression of the marriage vows
and must be willingly fruitful, we know that a child
is not conceived in every sexual union. God wills
this and has created the woman's body this way. As
the sovereign Lord of life, God ultimately determines which marital acts will result in the conception of a child. And spouses commit no evil by their
mutual decision to refrain from sexual union.

Based on these foundational principles, there is
a way for spouses to avoid conceiving a child due to
serious and just reasons and still engage in sexual
relations that are marital. It's called natural family
planning (NFP).

A woman's fertility cycle, which recurs about every twenty-eight days, can be divided into "phases." God has designed a woman's body in such a way that conception is possible during only one of these phases. Basically, NFP works to help the spouses detect when the woman has entered or has left her "fertile phase" by observing certain changes in her body. Spouses who for serious and just reasons wish to postpone pregnancy would abstain from all sexual relations during the woman's fertile phase and reserve their "lovemaking" for the infertile phases of the woman's cycle. This would be consistent with the foundational principles stated above because the spouses do not do anything directly to cause any sexual union to be infertile— they are just *naturally infertile*. This would be similar to spouses having sex who know that they are perpetually infertile (sterile), or when a woman is either in her post-child-bearing years or already pregnant. The Church has never said that it would be wrong for such people to have sex. Why? Because they haven't done anything *to make* their sexual acts infertile. The Church has also never said that the intention to avoid having children for a time due to serious and just reasons is a bad intention. In fact, it's a good one! Rather, the Church has said that the way in which spouses accomplish this must be compatible with the free, total, faithful, and fruitful love they expressed in their marriage vows, for they must always "tell the truth" with their bodies.

If spouses utilize NFP with pure hearts and the right intentions, their sexual union would still be *faithful* to their vows. It would be *free,* since NFP makes the decision when to have sex or not to have sex a deliberate one. It would be *total,* since NFP allows the spouses to offer their whole selves, even their fertility, in sexual union, even if it does not result in a child. It would be *willingly fruitful,* since if God willed the conception of a child as a result of any particular sexual union, the spouses would not have done anything to prevent this. By not directly causing their sexual union to be infertile, they are still indeed saying, "We may become parents—and we will it, if God wills it." All things considered, spouses who use NFP still love as God loves in and through their bodies.

Because spouses who utilize NFP have neither done anything to *make* their sexual acts infertile nor to directly eliminate the possibility of conception, they remain "open to life." This is what makes NFP very different from contraception. The way a couple actually avoids conception with NFP is by *abstaining from sexual relations.* When they do choose to engage in sexual relations, they do nothing to prevent the conception of a child if God wills it. Simply put, they haven't "contracepted" anything.[16]

In addition, NFP can actually help spouses who are having difficulty conceiving a child. By using NFP they can identify the woman's fertile phase and thereby significantly increase the chances of becoming pregnant. NFP is also instrumental in scientific advances, such as NaPro Technology (Natural Procreative Technology) developed by the Pope Paul VI Institute in Nebraska, which help couples to evaluate and treat a variety of women's health issues and conceive children when such conception was previously thought impossible. This leads to a very sensitive subject: infertility.

Infertility and the Call to Fruitfulness in Marriage

Before I continue I need to make clear that I empathize with the pain that infertile couples experience. My wife and I obviously have never had difficulty conceiving children. Yet, I have met numerous people in my life who have had such difficulty, even within my own family. You might also know someone who struggles with this. I have seen the pain and sorrow that comes from having an incredible desire to have children, yet for some reason not being able to. It is very heartbreaking to watch—I can't imagine what it's like to live through this.

Let me repeat that a couple that is *naturally* infertile, who through no deliberate choice is physically unable to bear children, does not have "less" of a marriage than a couple who has been blessed with many children. Neither is this couple "cursed" or "judged" by God as not deserving of children. In fact, as an image of the Trinity, their marriage is still called to be willingly fruitful. That's why the

Church encourages such couples to adopt children
or to offer themselves more fully to other work that
"fosters life," such as "various forms of educational
work, assistance to other families and to poor or
handicapped children" (John Paul II, *The Role of the
Christian Family in the Modern World*, no. 14).

This being said, in God's plan sexual union and
children go together and cannot be deliberately
separated from one another. Just as it is the case
with preventing pregnancy, it is also the case with
"achieving" pregnancy. Contracep-
tion and the like separate babies
from sex; in vitro fertilization, artificial insemination, and other replacement reproductive procedures separate sex from babies. Every child has
the right to be the fruit of the total self-
giving of his or her parents. Each has the
right to be conceived in love as the fruit
of the one flesh union of their mother and father.
Children are meant by God to be "begotten, not
made." They are meant to be received from him as a
gift. Nonmarital ways of conceiving human life,
even if done for the most altruistic of reasons, objectively change its creation from an act of *procreation*
into an act of *reproduction*. In *procreation*, the couple
acknowledges God as the Lord of life. In *reproduction*, parents and doctors *assume the role* of Lord of
life and treat the child as if he or she is a product to

> **For Your Consideration**
>
> These are procedures that "replace" sexual intercourse in order to conceive a child.

be manufactured. Besides this, many of the human beings made by in vitro fertilization are either killed or cryogenically frozen (for the couple to use in the future). The number of human beings "on ice" in laboratories all over the world is too high to count. Once the couple has had the number of children they desire, they usually either have their children destroyed or donated for research. These are just a few examples of how these technologies treat people as products—to be disposed of if they are no longer "useful."

However, I want to stress that *how* a person is conceived does not make him or her any more or less of a person. As Horton says in the story by Dr. Seuss, *Horton Hears a Who*, "a person's a person no matter how small," and, if I might add, *no matter how they were created*. It would be downright ridiculous to say that a child conceived by nonmarital acts, whether through in vitro fertilization or artificial insemination, or even fornication, adultery, or rape, are somehow less human or less valuable than anyone else. God is the Lord and Giver of life! All human beings are created by him in his image and have an eternal destiny. All human life is precious. All human life is sacred. All human life, no matter the circumstances in which it is created, ought to be celebrated. This is a given. But precisely because human life is so valuable, how it is created takes on such great importance.

• • • • •

In this chapter we have seen how God's plan for humanity is a "family plan." In fact, by his saving death and resurrection and his gift of the Spirit, Jesus has called all human beings to become part of God's family, the Church. And just as fathers and mothers are called to serve a natural family, priests and religious men and women are called to serve God's family.

JOHN PAUL II
In His Own Words

The fundamental task of the family is to serve life, to actualize in history the original blessing of the Creator [Gen 1:28]—that of transmitting by procreation the divine image from person to person.... However, the fruitfulness of conjugal [marital] love is not restricted solely to the procreation of children.... It is enlarged and enriched by all those fruits of moral, spiritual and supernatural life which the father and mother are called to hand on to their children, and through the children to the Church and to the world.

(The Role of the Christian Family in the Modern World, no. 28)

Things to Ponder and Share

1. How do you think the knowledge that spouses actually have of their mission to cooperate with God in enlarging and enriching his own family would affect the way couples view the procreation and education of children?

2. What ought to be the primary concern of parents regarding their children? Why?

3. What is a "contraceptive mentality"? How is it expressed today? How is abortion an extension of it?

4. How does a couple who has serious and just reasons to postpone conceiving a child respect their marriage vows when they use NFP, but not when they use contraception?

5. Why do replacement reproductive technologies, such as in vitro fertilization and artificial insemination, violate God's original plan for life, love, marriage, and sex?

6. Why is adoption and serving others such a rich part of our Church's teachings on the family?

7. Do you know any families that are truly "communities of life and love"? Describe the qualities that make them so.

Read the ———————————
Catechism of the Catholic Church

nos. 1655–1657, 2270-2275,
2366–2379

CHAPTER 17

The Final Chapter

Then I heard what seemed to be the voice of a great multitude, like the sound of many waters and like the sound of mighty thunderpeals, crying, "Hallelujah! For the Lord our God the Almighty reigns. Let us rejoice and exult and give him the glory, for the marriage of the Lamb has come, and his Bride has made herself ready; it was granted her to be clothed with fine linen, bright and pure"—for the fine linen is the righteous deeds of the saints. And the angel said to me, "Write this: Blessed are those who are invited to the marriage supper of the Lamb."

— Revelation 19:6–9

The Heavenly Marriage and the Celibate Life

In his popular book, *The Seven Habits of Highly Effective People,* Stephen Covey suggests that if a person is to be truly effective, whether in business or in life, then he or she must always "begin with the end in mind." Covey even goes so far as to ask his readers to imagine what they would want different people to say about them at their funeral.

Exercises like this, he believes, can help us to pin-point the sort of persons we should be each and every day. The Scriptures challenge us to do the same: "In all you do, remember the end of your life, and then you will never sin" (Sir 7:36).

Well, what is the "end" that we should keep in mind? It's our eternal destiny, of course! It's the meeting that each of us has with God at the "hour of our death." You see, the point of going back to "the beginning" isn't *only* so we can make ourselves ready to enter into an earthly marriage and enjoy earthly happiness. It's so we can make ourselves ready to enter into the *ultimate marriage* with God in heaven and enjoy eternal happiness! You could almost say that the real point of *The Cosmic Prequel* is to prepare for and get to *The Final Chapter:* our mar-riage with God!

Now, I know the whole idea of "marrying" God may sound a bit bizarre, but it's really not if you think about it. Didn't God teach Adam in his "lone-liness" that besides him there is "no other" and that every other "communion of persons" is secondary to the one with him? Didn't Jesus teach us that the first and greatest commandment is to love God with our whole heart, mind, soul, and strength (body), and then "our neighbor as ourselves"? Didn't St. Paul tell us that we "are not our own," that we belong to God and are called to become "one body" with him and "bear fruit"? I don't know about you, but this sounds an awful lot like marriage to me!

Marriage in Heaven?

So does that mean there is marriage in heaven as there is on earth? I think it's a perfectly natural thing for people to wonder about. The question itself reveals just how important marriage and sex are to us and how much happiness they bring when they are lived the way God intended. They are so important to us that we hope they last forever. They bring us so much happiness that we almost cannot conceive of heaven being without them and still being worthy of the name.

However, when seen in light of our ultimate "marriage" with God, it becomes clear that the answer is "no." When Jesus himself was asked the question: "Is there marriage in heaven as there is on earth?" he said that "in the resurrection they neither marry nor are given in marriage..." (Mt 22:30). At first, this may seem odd, or even harsh to us, especially considering that Jesus thought so highly of marriage that he took us back to "the beginning" to discover God's original plan for it. And yet, if you really think about God's original plan for life, love, marriage, and sex, it makes perfect sense.

While Jesus never excludes the possibility of having a unique relationship with your earthly spouse in heaven, he said "no" to there being marriage in heaven because he knew that *earthly marriage simply "pointed to" the marriage of God and his people.* He knew that earthly marriage was only a "sign" and a foretaste of what was in store for us when we entered the pearly gates. In fact, Jesus used the image of a wedding feast to describe heaven (Mt 25:1–13). And in the Scriptures, Jesus and his Father are identified as the Bridegroom (Mt 9:15; Jn 3:29; Is 54: 5, 62:5), and Israel, the Church, *and ourselves* as the Bride (Is 54:6; Jer 2:2; Song 4:8–12; Eph 5:22–23; Rev 19:7). So Jesus gave this answer because he understood that the "marriage" between God and us was the whole point of earthly marriage from "the beginning."

> **For Your Consideration**
>
> This is why the Church and the human soul (whether a woman's or a man's) are always referred to in the feminine.

Now, since there isn't marriage in heaven in the earthly sense, you may be wondering, "Is there sex in heaven?" Well, that all depends on what you mean by "sex." If by sex you mean "gender," there obviously *is* sex in heaven. In heaven we will be either male or female. This will be true *before* the resurrection of the dead, when our soul separates from our body and dwells with God, because our masculinity or femininity is not merely a biological reality, but also a spiritual one. It will certainly be true *after* our resurrection, when we are reunited with our bodies with all their masculine and feminine parts and become the body-persons God intended us to be from "the beginning."

And since we will be body-persons for all eternity, eternity will be a "body-soul" experience!

Heaven will not just be about a feeling of peace and fulfillment in our soul, but it will also be about the most radical bodily pleasure ever imagined! We will experience heaven with *our senses and our souls*. As I said earlier in the book, I firmly believe that heaven will have the most incredible sunsets, beautiful-smelling flowers, rockin' music, awesome ski slopes, and "wickedly" competitive baseball games ever dreamed of! Yet, they will all be clearly seen for what they are: expressions of God's free, total, faithful, and fruitful gift of himself to us. And they will be so dramatically better than their earthly counterparts that they will appear entirely new to us.

Although there will be sex in heaven in the sense of masculinity and femininity, and there will be the most radical bodily pleasure ever imagined, there *will not* be any sex in heaven in the sense of *sexual activity*. And simply put, this is because there *isn't* marriage in heaven in the way there is on earth.

When you think about it, the whole purpose of earthly marriage and marital sex will be rendered obsolete by our "marriage" with God in heaven. Sexual communion is a mere shadow of the communion with God for which we were all created. The "end of time" will mean the end of procreation as we know it, since body-persons are not created *in* heaven, but are created on earth *for* heaven. And the bliss of heaven will make even the most pleasurable sexual experience on earth seem like nothing in comparison. It can be likened to the difference between the pleasure derived from seeing a picture of an ice cream sundae and the pleasure derived from actually eating one...times about infinity!

Celibacy: The Heavenly Marriage "In Advance"

All of this discussion about our heavenly "marriage with God" should shed new light on the *celibate life.* So often celibacy is viewed as a cross that a man or woman must bear if they are to become a priest or religious brother or sister. If someone views it that way, then he or she *should not* become a priest or a religious brother or sister. The celibate life, properly understood, is not a rejection of marriage at all—it is a trading of earthly marriage for the heavenly marriage "in advance"! Celibacy is about giving oneself freely, totally, faithfully, and fruitfully to God—*the Bridegroom*—alone. It is about dedicating oneself completely to the Church—*the family of God*—and to building a culture of life and love. It is about making *vows to God* similar to the way spouses make vows to each other. Therefore, celibacy is, to a certain extent, a "living out" of the heavenly state while still on earth! (And, by the way, a *single person* could in fact be called to a life of celibacy without being called to the priesthood or religious life.)

Through a commitment to a life of prayer, a celibate man or woman devotes him- or herself to seeking the presence of God and forming a communion of persons with him on *this side of eternity.* And through a commitment to a life of service, a celibate man or woman devotes him or herself to loving as God loves in the most extremely inclusive way!

Notable Quotable

"The free choice of sacred celibacy...signifies a love without reservations; it stimulates to a charity which is open to all."
— Pope Paul VI

It must be admitted that, while the love of a husband and wife is called to be inclusive by accepting children lovingly from the Lord, spouses are rightly preoccupied with and focused on the good of each other and their children. In this sense, their "inclusiveness" is tempered by their state in life. As St. Paul said, "the married man is anxious about worldly affairs, how to please his wife...the married woman is anxious about worldly affairs, how to please her husband" (1 Cor 7:33–34). It would be wrong and irresponsible for a husband or a wife to be so involved in a ministry or a public service that they neglect the genuine needs of one another or their children. Married couples actually live out their baptismal call to love as God loves in and through their bodies by being a husband-father or wife-mother. Therefore, they need to be true to their state in life and the limits placed on it. St. Paul demanded this when he said, "Every one should remain in the state in which he was called" (1 Cor 7:20).

On the other hand, the love of a celibate man or woman is free from these constraints and therefore able to be more inclusive and universal in its scope. As St. Paul said, "The unmarried man is anxious about the affairs of the Lord...the unmarried woman is anxious about the affairs of the Lord, how to be holy in body and spirit..." (1 Cor 7:32, 34). Due to their state in life, celibate men and women are more available to serve God's people with abandon. Their love is fruitful and "gives life" to others, though in a different way from most married couples. For example, a priest gives supernatural life to others through Baptism, and a religious brother or sister gives life to others by, let's say, working with the poor or teaching the young.

It's important to note that those who enter the priesthood or religious life do not "check in" their masculinity or femininity at the door of the cathedral. They still have masculine and feminine gifts and corresponding masculine and feminine roles. You may not have ever thought about it, but there really is a reason we call them father, mother, sister, and brother. They serve the family of God, the Church, in a way similar to the way a father, mother, "older" sister or "older" brother serves their biological family.

It should also be noted that the family, in turn, serves the priesthood and religious life. The family is the rich soil in which religious vocations grow, for it is in the family that a person is formed in the faith, develops a love of prayer, and learns how to love as God loves by serving his or her parents and siblings.

So, *The Final Chapter* makes it clear that *marriage is for everyone* and that *marriage is the meaning of life!* God's original plan for life, love, marriage, and sex is the key to happiness—whether you are single, married, a priest, or a religious. Jesus reminded us of *The Cosmic Prequel,* bringing us "back to the beginning," so we could love as he loves in and through our bodies and fulfill the purpose of our existence. Treasure this truth; hold it close to your heart. I promise you that you will know a joy you never dreamed possible. You will also make yourself ready, not only for earthly marriage, but for the heavenly marriage to which you were called before the foundation of the world.

And I hope to see you there!

JOHN PAUL II
In His Own Words

When Christ spoke of the resurrection, he proved at the same time that the human body will also take part, in its way, in this eschatological [ultimate] experience of truth and love, united with the vision of God face to face. The human being, male and female, who, in the earthly situation where people usually marry (Lk 20:34), freely chooses [celibacy] for the kingdom of heaven, indicates that in that kingdom, which is the other world of the resurrection, people will no longer marry (Mk 12:25). This is because God will be "everything to everyone"(1 Cor 15:28).

(*GA*, 12/9/81 and 3/24/82)

Things to Ponder and Share

1. Name a time when "beginning with the end in mind" made you more effective and successful.
2. How does *The Cosmic Prequel* help us to prepare for and get to *The Final Chapter?*
3. How *is* there and *isn't* there marriage in heaven?
4. How *is* there and *isn't* there sex in heaven?
5. What do you imagine heaven will be like?
6. How does the celibate life anticipate the heavenly marriage rather than reject marriage as some think it does?

Read the ───────
Catechism of the Catholic Church

nos. 997–1001, 1023–1029,
1042–1050, 1060, 1612,
1618–1620, 2348–2349

Notes

1. These qualities of God's love are emphasized throughout the books *Good News about Sex & Marriage* (Servant Publications, 2000) and *Theology of the Body for Beginners* (Ascension Press, 2004), both by Christopher West.

2. William May, *An Introduction to Moral Theology* (Huntington, IN: Our Sunday Visitor, 1994), pp. 23–24.

3. These words are attributed to Samuel Smiles.

4. This is found in a famous work titled *Mere Christianity.*

5. Karol Wojtyla (Pope John Paul II), *Love and Responsibility* (New York: Farrar, Straus, & Giroux, 1981), p. 41.

6. See "Whatever Happened to Teen Romance? (And what is a friend with benefits, anyway?)" by Benoit Denizet-Lewis in *The New York Times Magazine,* May 30, 2004.

7. Vatican II, *Dogmatic Constitution on Divine Revelation,* n. 10.

8. St. John Damascene, *De fide orth.* 3, 24: PG 94,1089C, as cited in the *CCC,* no. 2559.

9. A paraphrase of St. Teresa of Avila, *The Book of Her Life,* 8, 5, in *The Collected Works of St. Teresa of Avila,* trans. K. Kavanaugh, OCD, and O. Rodriguez, OCD (Washington, DC: Institute of Carmelite Studies, 1976), I, 67, as cited in *CCC,* no. 2709.

10. Roy B. Zuck, *The Speaker's Quote Book* (Grand Rapids, MI: Kregel Publications, 1997), p. 242.

11. This insight is also made by Christopher West in his book *Theology of the Body for Beginners* (p. 91).

12. This is an excellent distinction made by Christopher West on p. 68 of his book *Good News About Sex & Marriage.* Some of my points about the difference between marital and nonmarital sex are also made by Mr. West on pp. 90–91 of this same book.

13. Pope John Paul II, *The Gospel of Life,* no. 13.

14. Paul VI, *Of Human Life,* no. 10. See also, "How should a couple discern 'just' and 'serious' reasons for postponing pregnancy?" from Jason Adams, *Called to Give Life* (Dayton, OH: One More Soul, 2003), pp. 123–128.

15. Vatican II, *Pastoral Constitution on the Church in the Modern World,* no. 50.

16. Christopher West, *Good News About Sex & Marriage: Answers to Your Honest Questions About Catholic Teaching* (Ann Arbor, MI: Servant Publications, 2000), p. 113.

Bibliography

Adams, Jason. *Called to Give Life*. Dayton, OH: One More Soul, 2003.

Aristotle. *Basic Works of Aristotle*. Ed. Richard McKeon. New York: Random House, Inc., 1941.

Benedict XVI. *God Is Love*. Boston: Pauline Books & Media, 2006.

Cantalamessa, Raniero. *Jesus Christ, the Holy One of God*. Collegeville, MN: The Liturgical Press, 1991.

Catechism of the Catholic Church. Libreria Editrice Vaticana, 1994.

Hogan, Rev. Richard, and Rev. John LeVoir. *Covenant of Love: Pope John Paul II on Sexuality, Marriage, and Family in the Modern World*. San Francisco: Ignatius Press, 1985.

John XXIII. *Christianity and Social Progress*. Vatican online translation, 1961.

John Paul II. *The Church: Mystery, Sacrament, Community*. Pauline Books & Media, 1998.

———. *The Gospel of Life*. Pauline Books & Media, 1995.

———. *The Role of the Christian Family in the Modern World*. Pauline Books & Media, 1981.

———. *The Theology of the Body: Human Love in the Divine Plan*. Pauline Books & Media, 1997.

May, William. *An Introduction to Moral Theology*. Huntington, IN: Our Sunday Visitor, 1994.

Paul VI. *Of Human Life*. Boston: Pauline Books & Media, 1968. Second Vatican Council. Dogmatic Constitution on the Church. Vatican online translation, 1964.

———. *Dogmatic Constitution on Divine Revelation*. Vatican online translation, 1965.

———. *Pastoral Constitution on the Church in the Modern World*. Vatican online translation, 1965.

West, Christopher. *Good News about Sex & Marriage: Answers to Your Honest Questions About Catholic Teaching*. Ann Arbor, MI: Servant Publications, 2000.

———. *Theology of the Body Explained: A Commentary of John Paul II's "Gospel of the Body."* Pauline Books & Media, 2003.

Wojtyla, Karol. *Love and Responsibility*. New York: Farrar, Straus, & Giroux, 1981.

Zuck, Roy, B.. *The Speaker's Quote Book*. Grand Rapids, MI: Kregel Publications, 1997.

DAVID HAJDUK is the Director of Campus Ministry and a member of the Religious Studies Department at Delbarton School in Morristown, New Jersey. He has over fifteen years of experience in religious education and youth ministry, which give David a keen awareness of the challenges facing young people in the twenty-first century. With two theology degrees as a foundation, David presents the Church's teaching in a fresh, engaging, and inspirational way, and has become a highly sought-after speaker on Pope John Paul II's *Theology of the Body.*

An accomplished guitarist and vocalist, David's moving, original songs on the themes of the *Theology of the Body* further the power of his gifted speaking

But David's best asset is that he is a husband and a father. He resides in Warren County, New Jersey, with his wife, Shannon, and their six children, whom they home-school.

To find out more about David Hajduk,
where he is appearing,
or to book one of his
dynamic presentations, visit...

davidhajduk.com

Pauline
BOOKS & MEDIA

The Daughters of St. Paul operate book and media centers at the following addresses. Visit, call or write the one nearest you today, or find us on the World Wide Web, www.pauline.org

CALIFORNIA

3908 Sepulveda Blvd, Culver City, CA 90230	310-397-8676
2460 Broadway Street, Redwood City, CA 94063	650-369-4230
5945 Balboa Avenue, San Diego, CA 92111	858-565-9181

FLORIDA

| 145 S.W. 107th Avenue, Miami, FL 33174 | 305-559-6715 |

HAWAII

| 1143 Bishop Street, Honolulu, HI 96813 | 808-521-2731 |
| Neighbor Islands call: | 866-521-2731 |

ILLINOIS

| 172 North Michigan Avenue, Chicago, IL 60601 | 312-346-4228 |

LOUISIANA

| 4403 Veterans Memorial Blvd, Metairie, LA 70006 | 504-887-7631 |

MASSACHUSETTS

| 885 Providence Hwy, Dedham, MA 02026 | 781-326-5385 |

MISSOURI

| 9804 Watson Road, St. Louis, MO 63126 | 314-965-3512 |

NEW JERSEY

| 561 U.S. Route 1, Wick Plaza, Edison, NJ 08817 | 732-572-1200 |

NEW YORK

| 64 W. 38th Street, New York, NY 10018 | 212-754-1110 |

PENNSYLVANIA

| 9171-A Roosevelt Blvd, Philadelphia, PA 19114 | 215-676-9494 |

SOUTH CAROLINA

| 243 King Street, Charleston, SC 29401 | 843-577-0175 |

VIRGINIA

| 1025 King Street, Alexandria, VA 22314 | 703-549-3806 |

CANADA

| 3022 Dufferin Street, Toronto, ON M6B 3T5 | 416-781-9131 |

¡También somos su fuente para libros,
videos y música en español!